HEARTS OF GOLD

A CELEBRATION OF SPECIAL OLYMPICS AND ITS HEROES

"You have come to be here in our little Bahamas this weekend to be brave enough to win and strong enough to compete with hearts of gold; you have done us an honor."

—*Sir Lynden Pindling,*
prime minister of the Bahamas
Opening Ceremonies of the first Special Olympics
Caribbean regional track and field meet
October 11, 1990

HEARTS OF

by **Sheila Dinn** with a foreword by Eunice Kennedy Shriver

GOLD

A CELEBRATION OF SPECIAL OLYMPICS AND ITS HEROES

Hearts of Gold *Advisory Committee*

Carol Caparosa Boland
Consultant for Grant Administration
Professional in the field of mental retardation

Andrea Cahn
Deputy Director of Public Affairs Department,
Special Olympics International

Loretta Claiborne
Special Olympics athlete
Special Olympics International board member

Teresa Fewel
Elementary school principal
Special Olympics International board member

Mark Hembd
Special Olympics athlete

Mike Hembd
Special Olympics athlete

Sandy Hembd
Parent of Special Olympics athletes
Original director of Families Program,
Special Olympics International

Stephen Malley
Senior Editor of Sports Illustrated
for Kids
Author of Sports Illustrated for Kids'
Guides to Olympic Games

Mary T. Meagher
Olympic gold medalist/swimming
Former Special Olympics International board
member

Dawn Munson
Director of Sports Publications & Research
Coordinator,
Special Olympics International

Sheila Young Ochowicz
Olympic gold medalist/speed skating
Former Special Olympics International board
member

Jim Santos
Director of Families Program,
Special Olympics International
Parent of Special Olympics athlete
Former Olympic track and field coach

Dr. Thomas Songster
Director of Sports, Training and Competition,
Special Olympics International

Delia Soto
Corporate Development Manager,
Special Olympics International

BLACKBIRCH PRESS, INC.
WOODBRIDGE, CT

To Loretta, Sandy, Mark, and Mike,
with thanks for helping me share your spirit.

The publisher would like to thank Jill Dixon, Andrea Cahn, and Lainey Canevaro at Special Olympics International for all their support and assistance with this book.

Grateful acknowledgment is made to Special Olympics International, Inc. for permission to use their name, logo, insignia, and other proprietary symbols throughout this publication.

The Special Olympics Logo, the terms Unified Sports®, and Partners Club® are trademarks of Special Olympics International, Inc.

Published by Blackbirch Press, Inc.
260 Amity Road
Woodbridge, CT 06525

© 1996 by Blackbirch Press, Inc.
Text © 1996 by Sheila Dinn
First Edition

Printed in Canada
10 9 8 7 6 5 4 3 2 1

Library of Congress Catalog-in-Publication Data

Dinn, Sheila.
    Hearts of Gold: a celebration of Special Olympics and its heroes/by Sheila
Dinn.—1st ed.
        p.   cm.
    Includes bibliographical references (p.   ) and index.
    Summary: Covers the history of the Special Olympics, the various events in which mentally and physically handicapped athletes compete, and some of the people involved in this international competition.
    ISBN 1-56711-163-7 (lib. bdg.)
    1. Special Olympics—Juvenile literature. 2. Physically handicapped athletes—Biography—Juvenile literature. [1. Special Olympics. 2. Athletes. 3. Handicapped.] I. Title.
GV722.5.S64D55 1996
796'.0196—dc20
                                       95-35834
                                          CIP
                                          AC

Cover Photo Credits
On the front cover: *top left*, Eric Tosado, 1987 World Games (Special Olympics International); *top middle*, Thomas Edmonds, 1995 World Games (Bruce Glassman); *top right*, two runners, 1990 European Games (Special Olympics International); *middle*, swimmer, 1995 World Games (Special Olympics International); *bottom*, skater, 1993 World Winter Games (Special Olympics International).
On the back cover: *top left*, Mikhail Zhirov, 1995 World Games (Bruce Glassman); *top right*, New Haven stands, Opening Ceremonies, 1995 World Games (Special Olympics International/Margolis); *bottom left*, father and son, 1987 World Games (Special Olympics International); *bottom right*, skiier, 1989 World Winter Games (Special Olympics International).
On the title page: stands in New Haven, 1995 World Games (Bruce Glassman).

CONTENTS

As I read through all of the stories of Special Olympics and Olympic heroes in this book, I thought of the many different kinds of "success" they demonstrate. Many earned gold medals in their sport or fame in their town or country. Some ran faster or jumped farther than anyone ever had before. Some of the athletes felt it was important to use their talent to help or teach others. And many simply show us how they do their best with the skills they have.

Like the athletes in this book, every Special Olympics athlete lives out the word *success*. Mastering four strokes to swim the 400-meter individual medley or improving basic motor skills to compete in a 15-meter flotation race—both are success. Learning the rules and strategies and teamwork it takes to play basketball or overcoming the nervous feeling of leaving home for the State Games—both are success. Simply not accepting the limitations that the world may put on people with disabilities—that is success.

For if there is one thing that Special Olympics athletes know, it's that it is what a person has inside that matters. That's what the stories in this book show us. But believe me—these stories are only the tip of the iceberg. This spirit is shared by hundreds of thousands of Special Olympics athletes around the world—and by their families, coaches, and friends.

Ever since the first Special Olympics Games in 1968, Special Olympics athletes have said to the world, "Do you see what we can do?" They want the chance to explain their training schedules—how they work so hard to meet their goals and demand the best of their bodies and minds. They want the world to see the great joy that they take in competing well, in sharing their skills with friends and family, in simply being able to participate.

Why?

Because Special Olympics athletes want the world to take it all in and say, "Yes, we see! If they can do all this, then they can be good workers, good students, good neighbors! Our doors will be open to them."

More and more doors *are* opening for people with mental retardation. More and more people *do* understand about their many different abilities. In the decades since we began to provide sports opportunities for people with mental retardation, much *has* changed.

But we still have far to go.

This book is a chance for Special Olympics sports heroes to tell their stories—to shout out to the world and show their spirit. If you are a Special Olympics athlete, you feel that spirit. Whatever you do, do it well! If you are just learning about Special Olympics from this book, I hope you will go out and see a Special Olympics event for yourself. I hope you will meet athletes and their families and celebrate their success! I hope you will open your door to people with mental retardation!

And open your heart to their hearts of gold.

Eunice K Shriver

Eunice Kennedy Shriver

Olympic winners in ancient Greece were crowned with wreaths of olive branches.

An Olympic History

The Ancient Olympic Games

Imagine sitting on a hill overlooking a field of grass. Groves of olive trees surround the scene, and rocky mountain peaks rise to the blue sky. You and a crowd of thousands watch as young men gather at the starting line and race 600 feet on the field below you. You cheer as the winner is crowned with a wreath woven from wild olive branches. The winner is a hero. You and your friends celebrate and dream of wearing a champion's crown someday. Where are you? You are in Olympia, Greece, the site of the ancient Olympic Games. The time is some 2,500 years ago—about the year 500 B.C. The Games you are watching are the beginning of the Olympic Games we know today.

The first written record of the ancient Olympic Games is in the year 776 B.C. The Games began with a single event, the 600-foot (183-meter) stade (stadium) race, held along with religious ceremonies and celebrations. In the ancient Greeks' religion, there were many gods and goddesses. The king of them all was Zeus. Zeus was pleased by excellence, by good competition, and by winning. To honor Zeus and make him happy, the Greeks decided to bring together their best athletes for a competition and festival.

They chose the place called Olympia because it was important in their religion and because it had a good field for races and a hill for spectators. That's why the

9

The history of the Christian world is divided into two time periods. "B.C." means "before Christ." For this time period years are counted backward from the year when Jesus Christ is said to have been born. The time after Jesus Christ was born is "A.D.," short for a Latin phrase that means "in the year of our Lord." A.D. years are counted forward.

event came to be called the Olympic Games. The Games were held every four years from 776 B.C. to 393 A.D.—293 times in all!

Greece was made up of city-states, which were almost like separate countries. The city-states often fought against each other, but every four years all wars stopped during the Olympic Games. People traveled from all over Greece and the Greek colonies to compete in and watch the Games. The athletes who competed worked hard and were honored by their towns and city-states, just like our sports stars are today.

In those days, no women were allowed to compete in the Games, or even watch them! Different events were added as the Games continued through the years, including other foot races, chariot races, horse races, wrestling, and boxing.

By 393 A.D., Greece had become part of the Roman Empire, and the Empire had made Christianity its official religion. That meant no more festivals for Zeus—and no more Olympic Games.

Fast Forward: 1896

With no more festivals, the Games site at Olympia was soon overgrown, covered by mud from a flood, and broken up by earthquakes. Centuries passed. No one knew about the place or the Olympic Games until around the year 1800. Then, archaeologists discovered the big stone Temple of Zeus at Olympia. For the next 100 years, archaeologists and historians uncovered more buildings and learned about the ancient Olympic Games.

Pierre de Coubertin, a wealthy baron (or nobleman) from France, was very interested in these discoveries. He liked what the ancient Olympic Games stood for: sports, healthy bodies, and peace. He thought those ideals would be good for the modern world. So he gathered together people who loved sports and led them in organizing the first modern Olympic Games in Athens, Greece, in 1896.

The Olympic Games have been held every four years since then, except in times of war. Winter Games were added in 1924. As of 1994, Winter Games are held two years before each Summer Games, instead of both Winter and Summer Olympic Games being held during the same year. Women competed as of 1900—but only in the "ladylike" sports of tennis and golf. They swam as of 1912 and competed in track in 1928.

The worldwide Olympic movement is led by the International Olympic Committee (IOC), which has its

"Running keeps my mind clear and my body fit. I like the competition, but I also get a good feeling when I see other people win."

—Chris Byrne,
Special Olympics athlete

Crowds cheer the winner of the marathon race at the first modern Olympic Games in Athens, 1896.

headquarters in Geneva, Switzerland. The IOC decides where each Olympic Games will be held. There is also a national Olympic committee in each country to organize that nation's athletes for the Olympic Games.

Baron de Coubertin started the modern Olympics to bring together the best athletes in the world in different sports. These athletes had to be dedicated to their sport and to being the best. When the modern Games began, the athletes had to be amateurs—that is, they could not be paid for training and competing in their sport. That rule changed recently and now professional athletes may compete in most of the sports at the Olympic Games.

Just like in ancient Greece, modern Olympic athletes are heroes in their towns and countries. They train hard and dream of winning a gold medal. They want to live up to the Olympic motto: "Citius, Altius, Fortius," which is Latin for "Faster, Higher, Stronger." They want to do their best.

Chapter 2

Special Olympics is a worldwide sports training and competition program for people with mental retardation. Special Olympics began more than 25 years ago.

Eunice Kennedy Shriver and her brother, President John F. Kennedy, worked together to change the lives of people with mental retardation.

The Story of Special Olympics

 Athletes around the world share the Olympic dream of running the fastest, jumping the highest, and proving they are the strongest. But for a long time, people with mental retardation could not share that dream because there was no chance for them to participate in sports.

Until about 30 years ago, doctors and other experts thought that people with mental retardation weren't strong enough or clever enough to play sports and that physical activity was dangerous to their health. At that time, most people with mental retardation in the United States and other developed countries lived in institutions rather than with their families. Most institutions were more like hospitals than homes, keeping people with disabilities away from the rest of the world. People who lived in institutions did not have activities to help either their minds or bodies learn and grow. This meant that most people with mental retardation had no chance to gain strength in their muscles or to become physically fit.

Welcome to Camp Shriver

In the early 1960s, all that began to change. In 1962, Eunice Kennedy Shriver, whose brother John F. Kennedy was then the president of the United States, wrote a magazine article announcing that her sister Rosemary had mental retardation.

Mental retardation is a difference in thinking and understanding that can mean a person learns at a slower pace than others of his or her age. There are an estimated 7.5 million people with mental retardation in the United States, and an estimated total of 190 million in the world.

There are many different causes of mental retardation, and there are also many different levels of learning ability. Some people with mental retardation may also have a physical disability.

This made a huge difference in the way other families who had a child with mental retardation felt. Suddenly, it wasn't something to be so ashamed of!

The Kennedy family donated money from the Joseph P. Kennedy, Jr. Foundation—named after a brother who had been killed in World War II—to help improve the lives of people with mental retardation. Mrs. Shriver got the president to support a new program of physical fitness tests for people with mental retardation. She also started a summer day camp at her home in Maryland, USA to provide a place for people with mental retardation to learn and play sports.

Unlike most doctors of that time, Mrs. Shriver believed that a person with mental retardation could enjoy and benefit from physical activity. Growing up, she had watched Rosemary play along with the rest of the family. The nine Kennedy brothers and sisters loved competing with each other, especially in sports, and Rosemary had kept up with most of their activities.

In the summer of 1962, 100 young people with mental retardation came to Mrs. Shriver's camp to run, swim, play soccer, and ride horses. They enjoyed the camp and loved the sports they learned, and by the end of the summer they were "faster and stronger" than ever before. The doctors and experts had been wrong!

The camp proved another important thing: that people with and without mental retardation could get along and become friends. Local high school and college students had helped to teach and coach the campers after attending evening

Young people exercise in the open air at Camp Shriver.

training sessions for one month before the camp started. The young *volunteers* loved the experience—and to this day, Special Olympics relies on volunteers to run training and competition programs around the world.

After 1962, programs like Camp

Shriver were started at parks and other places around the United States and Canada. The Kennedy Foundation helped fund many of these sports camps.

The city of Chicago, Illinois, USA had an especially strong program, with a lot of participants and volunteers. In 1967, the people who ran the Chicago program decided that athletes from around the city were ready to compete against one another. When they asked the Kennedy Foundation for money to help organize a city-wide competition, Mrs. Shriver decided to take the idea even further—and hold an international competition! The time had finally come for the hard work and high hopes of athletes with mental retardation to be recognized.

"The World Will Never Be the Same"

In 1968, Mrs. Shriver, the Kennedy Foundation, and Chicago's Parks Department organized the First Special Olympics World Games. One thousand athletes with mental retardation from the United States and Canada arrived in Chicago on July 20. The next morning the athletes gathered at Chicago's famous football stadium, Soldier Field.

There were only a few people in the stands along with Mrs. Shriver and several well-known Olympic and professional athletes who already saw how important Special Olympics would be to people with mental retardation. But the small number of fans didn't make it any less thrilling for the athletes as they paraded into the stadium behind a bright blue and gold flag—their flag.

Eunice Shriver remembers the excitement that filled Soldier Field that morning. "My best memory is watching the athletes march in," she said. "Chicago's mayor, Richard Daley, leaned over as we watched and said, 'Eunice, the world will never be the same again.' How right he was!"

Mrs. Shriver continued: "I knew that it was those athletes who had done more to start Special Olympics than anyone. They were driven by desire and knowledge—they knew they

" . . . it was those athletes who had done more to start Special Olympics than anyone. . . . "

—Eunice Shriver, speaking about the Special Oympics athletes from the first Games in 1968

could do sports, and if they could, why not do it in a huge way? Why couldn't they be doing it all over the country, all over the world?

"If those athletes had been uninterested or bored, Special Olympics probably never would have happened. You can't push people into something like this—their enthusiasm has to carry it. Young people everywhere

Top: Eunice Shriver (right) joins athletes exercising at the 1968 Games. Bottom: Winners stand tall at Soldier Field, in Chicago.

Shown here with Olympic gymnast Bart Conner, Mike Stone (right) competed in the first Games in 1968.

should understand that. It's when they throw themselves into something that it gets bigger. They are in control."

Mike Stone was one of the Special Olympics athletes at the Games in 1968. He had traveled from his home state of North Carolina, USA with three other athletes and their coaches. None of them had ever been on a plane before. The athletes stayed in one of Chicago's nicest hotels—another first for most of the athletes. Mike was thrilled by the trip.

"All I can say is, it was amazing," said Mike. "I was twelve years old and we knew we were the luckiest athletes to be chosen to go to the Games. What a time we had! Meeting new friends, learning skills from coaches, just learning a lot of things from a lot of people.

"I've been to four international Special Olympics Games now. The Games have gotten much larger. Now athletes around the world all have a chance to show who they are, and what they believe in." Mike's most recent trip to World Games was to the 1995 Summer Games in Connecticut, USA. The 39-year old won a silver in his division of 18-hole golf.

"Now athletes around the world all have a chance to show who they are, and what they believe in."

—Mike Stone, Special Olympics athlete

Mike also contributes money to his local Special Olympics program from his job as a custodian with the U.S. Postal Service. His whole family joins him in volunteering for Special Olympics.

Around the Clock, Around the World

Those First International Special Olympics Games in Chicago were the beginning of the official history of Special Olympics. Since 1968, millions of people with mental retardation have trained and competed in sports through Special Olympics! Today, athletes in more than 140 countries participate. You could even say that "the sun never sets on Special Olympics" since at every hour of every day, someone is training somewhere in the world!

The growth of Special Olympics is exciting because it shows how people with mental retardation all over the world have more and more opportunity to learn, to dream, and to achieve. In the United States, for example, people with disabilities

From African villages to major cities, Special Olympics athletes proudly march in their Parade of Athletes.

are now included in regular school and sports programs as much as possible. Special Olympics adds to these opportunities with the fast-growing Unified Sports® and Sports Partnership programs. (See pages 23–25.)

The Ninth Special Olympics World Summer Games were held in July 1995 in New Haven, Connecticut, USA. The size and success of these Games show how much Special Olympics has grown since 1968. At the 1995 World Games, 7,000 athletes competed instead of the 1,000 who had competed in 1968. More than 100,000 spectators and family members attended, instead of just a handful. Athletes competed in 19 sports, instead of just track and swimming as they had in Chicago in 1968.

But some things were the same: The Special Olympics flag still waved, telling the world about the joy of sports and the thrill of doing your best. The Special Olympics Flame of Hope burned in a cauldron from the beginning to the end of Games. And the Special Olympics Oath inspired the athletes and all who watched them:

> "Let me win, but if I cannot win,
> let me be brave in the attempt."

Chapter 3

Special Olympics conducts training and competition programs around the world.

Athletes in the former Soviet Union learn skiing skills.

How Special
Olympics Works

Special Olympics athletes can be as young as eight or as old as 99! They live in countries all over the world—Australia, the United States, India, China, Peru, Zimbabwe, and many more. Athletes join a local Special Olympics program through a community organization or school and choose a sport to train in, or one sport for each season. The 22 sports that Special Olympics offers include summer and winter sports and individual and team sports.

The athletes practice hard to prepare for Special Olympics Games. These games include: local, area or county, state or regional, and national games (outside the United States) and, every two years, World Winter or Summer Games. Every Special Olympics Games begins with a Parade of Athletes, the Special Olympics Oath, and the lighting of a cauldron with the Special Olympics Flame of Hope.

Volunteers keep all of the Games running smoothly. Many different kinds of people volunteer for Special Olympics: students; athletes' family members and friends; businesspeople; and sports leaders and athletes from professional, high school, and college teams. There are also trained officials for every event because Special Olympics athletes must follow the rules of their sport just like athletes in any sports program.

Practice, Practice, Practice!

Because there are both summer and winter Special Olympics Games (as well as fall and spring tournaments in most areas), Special Olympics athletes can choose from different sports for each season of the year. Each season, athletes work with a volunteer coach for at least eight weeks (or 12 training sessions) before competing in that sport.

First, Special Olympics coaches learn about the sport they will coach and the coaching skills that will help them teach athletes with mental retardation. Then, with the help of a Sports Skills Guide that Special Olympics headquarters has written for each of its sports, the coach makes a plan for the eight weeks of training.

Training programs can include anywhere from one to five practices per week. As the weeks go by, the athletes learn more and more complicated skills. For winter sports such as figure skating and Alpine skiing, athletes will have some training on the ice or snow, but they may also practice skills and do *fitness conditioning* off of the ice or snow. If it's a

A shining moment for any Special Olympics athlete: carrying the Flame of Hope.

team sport, they go from learning basic skills to team practice and game situations. The coach finds a position for each athlete where he or she feels comfortable and can contribute to the team. Teamwork is a big part of team sports, but athletes in individual sports practice teamwork too, by cheering each other on and challenging each other to improve.

Each training session includes most of these things:
- warm-up and stretching exercises;
- physical conditioning, like running or strength exercises;
- talks about the sport, rules, equipment, competitions, and *sportsmanship*;
- instruction and practice in sports skills;
- team play if it's a team sport; and
- scrimmages or practice competitions within the training group.

Many Special Olympics athletes add their own training time to the group practices they attend each week. Runners may train with a local running club. Athletes who compete in bowling and powerlifting may put in extra time at the bowling lanes or gym with friends or fellow athletes. Members of a team can get together for fitness training or scrimmages.

Another way that athletes get extra practice in their sport is through Family Home Training. This program helps families work on the sports skills that their athletes have learned at Special Olympics practice. Coaches give out a Family Home Training packet that lists exercises and practice drills for the athlete to work on at home. Athletes can keep their "scores" on a poster as they improve their skills each week. Family Home Training is just one of the important ways that families contribute to their athletes' success in Special Olympics.

At the end of the eight-week training session, each Special Olympics athlete is ready for competition. The athlete's excitement and motivation has been building right along with sports skills and fitness—and he or she wants to reach for the top! After the competition, the athlete may be chosen to compete at the next level of Special Olympics Games. Most athletes then choose a sport for the next season and keep training. After all, Special Olympics goes on all year, all around the world!

World-famous football (soccer) clinician Hubert Vogelsinger demonstrates for athletes at the 1995 World Games.

A Fair Chance to Win

Special Olympics is open to all individuals with mental retardation, so there is a wide range of skills and abilities among the athletes. At Special Olympics Games, athletes and teams are placed in divisions so that they compete against others of similar age and ability. This makes Special Olympics different from the Olympic Games and many other sports programs, in which only the best athletes can compete and win. In Special Olympics, each division is an event of its own, not a *heat* where only the winner advances to the finals. This gives each athlete a fair chance to win and to feel that he or she has succeeded.

Here's how ability divisions work in an event like the 100-meter dash: Each Special Olympics athlete who is

WORLD GAMES

Year	Place	Number of Athletes	Number of Participating Countries
Summer Games			
1968	Chicago, Illinois, USA	1,000 athletes	2 countries
1970	Chicago, Illinois, USA	2,000 athletes	3 countries
1972	Los Angeles, California, USA	2,500 athletes	3 countries
1975	Mt. Pleasant, Michigan, USA	3,200 athletes	15 countries
1979	Brockport, New York, USA	3,500 athletes	24 countries
1983	Baton Rouge, Louisiana, USA	4,000 athletes	51 countries
1987	South Bend, Indiana, USA	4,700 athletes	70 countries
1991	Minneapolis/St. Paul, Minnesota, USA	6,000 athletes	100 countries
1995	New Haven, Connecticut, USA	7,000 athletes	147 countries
Winter Games			
1977	Steamboat Springs, Colorado, USA	500 athletes	2 countries
1981	Smuggler's Notch & Stowe, Vermont, USA	600 athletes	11 countries
1985	Park City, Utah, USA	825 athletes	14 countries
1989	Reno, Nevada & Squaw Valley, California, USA	1,000 athletes	18 countries
1993	Salzburg & Schladming, Austria	1,551 athletes	51 countries

training in the 100-meter dash is timed before going to a competition. The games organizers take all of the runners' times and divide the athletes into groups of eight or fewer athletes with similar times. (Eight is the common number of lanes on a track or in a pool, so that number was chosen as the number of competitors or teams in a division for all sports.)

At Special Olympics Games, from local games to the World Games, there will be many 100-meter races run. In one, the athletes may finish in 30 seconds. In another, runners may cross the finish line in 14 seconds or less.

The first National Games in China marked a new era in the lives of people with disabilities in that country.

After each race, the first, second, and third place winners of that race are awarded gold, silver, and bronze medals, and each of the other runners receives a ribbon for the place he or she finished. (At local games, the first three finishers often receive a ribbon instead of a medal.)

The medal winners from any of these races—the fastest race, slowest race, or any race in between—may then be chosen to represent their Special Olympics program at the next level of games, like the State, National, or World Special Olympics Games.

Building Basic Skills

Some athletes with mental retardation have more serious physical disabilities that don't allow them to participate in regular training and competition. Special Olympics has another opportunity for these athletes, called the Motor Activities Training Program, or MATP.

In the MATP, trained coaches lead athletes in group games and activities that help build basic *motor skills*. After eight weeks, the athletes take part in a Training Day, which may be held along with local Special Olympics Games, and they receive Challenge Medals to recognize their hard work and improvement.

Some MATP athletes improve in their motor skills enough to move on to regular competition events for athletes of lower ability levels. For example, an athlete may compete in the 10-meter assisted walk event or the 15-meter flotation race. These events are held during Special Olympics Games, and the athletes earn medals or ribbons. Other athletes may remain in the MATP and continue to work on activities at their own ability level.

A Unifying Force

Special Olympics organizes Unified Sports® programs that bring together athletes with and without mental retardation to play on the same teams, against other Unified Sports® teams in competitive leagues. Unified Sports® began in basketball, softball, soccer, volleyball, distance running, and bowling. Now Unified Sports® programs are run in all Special Olympics sports—golf, skiing, you name it! The program may be part of a school sports program or a town's recreation program.

Unified Sports® helps athletes with mental retardation improve their skills and learn more about sports opportunities outside of Special Olympics. These programs also open the eyes of non–Special Olympics athletes (called Partners) to the abilities of their new friends. Partners may start out wondering how they will relate to Special Olympics athletes, but before long, they're all going out for pizza!

"The Special Olympics athletes are very similar to other high school students. They work very hard and they want to be successful."

*—Michael Dedmond,
Unified Sports® coach*

The Connecticut Unified softball team shows its unity at the 1995 World Games.

Unified Sports® has quickly become very popular in the United States, and new programs are thriving in Europe, the Middle East, the Caribbean Islands, and South and Central America. In the former Soviet Union, many Special Olympics organizers have caught the excitement and are bringing athletes with and without mental retardation together in places where, a few years ago, most people would not acknowledge anyone with a disability.

Robert "Beau" Doherty, executive director of Connecticut Special Olympics, was one of the first to see the importance of the Unified Sports® concept, and sees it becoming even more important in the future. "I see Unified Sports® as the biggest program of Special Olympics' future. There is nothing that has a better track record of bonding athletes with and without mental retardation in a way that promotes understanding and acceptance in the realm of sports."

Mark Stry is a Special Olympics athlete who competed in Unified basketball at Central High School in Evansville, Indiana, USA. He knows what he likes about Unified basketball! "I feel excitement and enthusiasm when the crowd is cheering for me. I like being with my friends and competing with them," said Mark.

Central High School has three Unified basketball teams, each led by one of the school's varsity (American) football coaches. This means that there is strong competition among the teams, but also a lot of friendship. Ron Kane, who coached Mark Stry's basketball team, sees Unified Sports® as an important way for athletes with mental retardation and their teammates to learn about each other. Coach Michael Dedmond, who was an all-star athlete when he was in high school, considers coaching Unified Sports® one of his most rewarding experiences. "The Special Olympics athletes are very similar to the other high school students," said Michael. "They work very hard and they want to be successful. I have also found that the higher my expectations, the more the athletes produce. All our teams play hard, but we try to show sportsmanship in winning and losing."

Washington Middle School in Evansville also has Unified basketball. Seventh-grader Brandon Robbins said that one important thing he learned by playing was that "special ed students are not really so different from everyone else. They don't all have to be treated special."

Special Olympics has two other programs to promote *inclusion*. Sports Partnerships match up a Special Olympics athlete with a varsity or junior varsity athlete in a school, and the athletes train together for their sports season. In Partner Clubs®, a student without mental retardation teams up with a Special Olympics athlete for sports and social activities.

Nations Gathering in Peace

Every two years, thousands of proud athletes from all over the world gather for Special Olympics World Games, alternating between summer and winter. The athletes try hard to win a medal. They are also thrilled to travel, to meet people from other countries, and to make new friends. Along with great competition, the Games feature parties and dances for athletes and families, an Olympic Town with fun and educational activities, and plenty of opportunities to learn about other cultures and other sports. Many famous people in sports, entertainment, and government come to the World Games to meet Special Olympics athletes and to show their support for Special Olympics programs. This makes the Games even more exciting!

In the words of Special Olympics athlete Pavo Straka, a cross-country skier from Slovakia, "I admire 'terminator' Arnold Schwarzenegger. It was for me a miracle to embrace him in Schladming during the Opening Ceremonies of the World Winter Games in 1993."

Pavo was one of the competitors at the Fifth Special Olympics World Winter Games, which were held in the country of Austria. The town of Schladming, famous for its ski slopes, hosted the ski events. The city of Salzburg hosted the skating and hockey events. The 1993 Winter Games were the first Special Olympics World Games to be held outside the United States.

Read on to find out about the latest World Games!

Special Olympics athletes and their families come from around the world to attend the World Games.

Chapter 4

Special Olympics sports programs change athletes' lives every day. World Games give Special Olympics athletes a chance to change the world with their skill, courage, sharing, and joy.

Eunice Kennedy Shriver and Sargent Shriver speak at the Closing Ceremonies of the 1995 World Games.

A Week of Spirit and Splendor

The Yale Bowl Stadium in New Haven, Connecticut, USA is usually home to college athletes, or maybe an occasional touring soccer team. On the night of July 1, 1995, it was home to a world: a world of heroes and their hopes; a world of believers and their dreams. It was home to 7,000 Special Olympics athletes and the coaches and families who stand behind them.

On that night, the Yale Bowl hosted the Opening Ceremonies of the 1995 Special Olympics World Summer Games. Along with the athletes and coaches, some 70,000 spectators filled the stands. Celebrities led each delegation into the stadium as the crowd roared. Top men and women from world governments shared the stage with Eunice Kennedy Shriver and her husband Sargent.

The crowd stilled as Special Olympics athlete Loretta Claiborne stood at the microphone to introduce the president of the United States, Bill Clinton. Later Loretta would say, "Introducing the president was fine, but I'd rather introduce Eunice." And after Clinton spoke, Loretta did just that.

People in the stands listened as the founder of Special Olympics spoke. "I say to you, our Special Olympians, you are the heroes and heroines who have overcome. So go home and tell your countrymen, 'I am a champion athlete—and I represented my nation before all the world. Train me for work I can do. Grant me my humanity. I have talent—priceless and precious. I will never give in!'"

More than 40,000 volunteers helped the athletes turn in top performances.

The evening ended in grand style, as Connecticut Special Olympics sailing athlete Kathy Ledwidge and her Unified Partner Mark Chanski together held the Flame of Hope to the cauldron that would burn throughout the week. The Games had begun!

These were the biggest Special Olympics Games ever, and the biggest sporting event in the world in 1995. They will be remembered for all the firsts that happened in New Haven. The list of national Special Olympics programs competing in Summer Games for the first time numbered 40 of the 147 total. New delegations came from countries such as South Africa, Mali, Finland, Qatar, and Ukraine. Of the 19 sports contested at the Games, golf, sailing, and badminton appeared for the first time. Many sports had new and more difficult events: the 100-meter and 110-meter hurdles and the 26.2-mile marathon in athletics; the 40-kilometer (26-mile) road race in cycling; and the squat in powerlifting.

These were the first World Games in which most of the sports included Unified events. On the Yale Bowl field, hundreds of athletes without mental retardation

Fans spelled out country names in one of the largest and most complex card displays ever.

Athletes young and old, 15,000 family members, and hundreds of thousands of spectators enjoyed the 1995 World Games.

stood with their Special Olympics teammates and friends, ready to compete. The 1995 Games also brought the Athletes as Officials program to a world stage. Among the 1,100 certified officials who traveled from 60 countries to preside over the events, 50 were Special Olympics athletes who had passed all of the tests necessary to officiate in their chosen sport!

For the first time at a Special Olympics Summer Games, more than 5,000 athletes and coaches from outside the United States came to the country early and lived in some 1,000 private homes in towns across Connecticut. For three days before moving into Games housing in New Haven, athletes from as far away as Tanzania and Armenia, Luxemborg and the Philippines enjoyed family meals, festive town picnics, and practice time at high schools and YMCAs. For many of the athletes who live in institutions, this was their first time in a family home! All of the athletes loved it—but judging by the way the townspeople cheered for their new friends at their competitions, and the number of them planning trips to the countries they'd learned about, perhaps the hosts loved it more!

As the week came to an end, athletes prepared for the final event—the first-ever Special Olympics marathon. Along with the 19 marathoners were the 47 competitors in the half marathon and the 16 Unified marathon and half marathon runners.

"I say to you, our Special Olympians, . . . go home and tell your countrymen, 'I am a champion athlete—and I represented my nation before all the world. Train me for work I can do. Grant me my humanity.' . . ."

—Eunice Kennedy Shriver, founder of Special Olympics, at the Opening Ceremonies for the 1995 World Games

And when the race was run, Pennsylvanian Troy Rutter's winning time of 2:59.18 (which would have won the Olympic marathon in 1900 and 1904!) stood as a terrific symbol for all of the athletic accomplishments of the Games: athletes turning in personal bests; athletes stunning officials and spectators with their skills; athletes on sports pages and evening news programs all around the world; athletes showing that there are no limits to what a person with mental retardation can do, with training, practice, and determination.

As the cauldron's flame slowly died at the Closing Ceremonies on July 9, those 7,000 athletes turned to face the world again—with medals and memories to last a lifetime.

Chapter 5

*Olympic spirit
is shared by
athletes of the
Olympic Games
and of Special
Olympics.*

**This moment of
victory lasts a
lifetime.**

Sharing the Olympic Spirit

Having the word *Olympics* in its name means that Special Olympics shares important qualities with the Olympic Games, in which the best athletes from around the world compete. Like the Olympic Games, Special Olympics brings nations and people together in peace, in the name of sports, and sportsmanship. In 1987, the International Olympic Committee (IOC) recognized Special Olympics as a valuable worldwide sports program for people with mental retardation that also upholds the philosophy of the Olympic Games. With this official recognition, the IOC allows Special Olympics to use the word *Olympics*. The National Olympic Committees in many countries, including the United States, also support national Special Olympics programs.

While Special Olympics and Olympic Games are alike in many ways, there are also obvious differences between the two. For the Olympic Games, the world's best athletes train for years to reach the highest level in their sport and to be chosen to represent their countries. Then the Games bring these athletes together to find out who really is the best.

Special Olympics, on the other hand, offers ongoing sports training for people with mental retardation so that they can learn and compete in sports. The athletes also learn discipline and fitness habits to help them in other parts of their lives.

Each training program leads to a competition where the athletes try their best to win. But the athletes also realize the importance of working hard and improving their times and scores.

The important thing that the athletes of the Olympic Games and of Special Olympics have in common is the Olympic spirit. This is the feeling inside an athlete that tells her to keep trying and keep working because she knows she can be better. It's what makes runners shake hands at the starting line and congratulate each other at the finish line.

Olympic skier Billy Kidd coaches a Special Olympics athlete at the first World Winter Games in 1977.

Special Olympics medalists like this woman become hometown heroes after World Games.

The Olympic spirit is what makes a member of a team willing to sit on the sideline when someone else is playing better and will help the team win. It's being proud to represent your town and your country and doing your best to make your town and country proud of you. The Olympic spirit is something that all true athletes have inside themselves. It is what the whole world celebrates during both the Olympic Games and the Special Olympics Games.

"I admire Jackie Joyner-Kersee . . . She has influenced me to do my best, whether I win or lose, and to be thankful that I have the chance to be part of a sporting event."

—Kristen Doherty,
Special Olympics athlete

Special Olympics winter sports bring athletes to the challenges of tough ski slopes, winding cross-country courses, and rinks waiting for both art and speed!

Cross-country skiers glide through the trees at the first World Winter Games in 1977.

From Mountain to Rink

 ## Alpine Skiing

Picture the scene: a snow-covered mountain at Steamboat Springs, Colorado, USA in February 1977 . . . dozens of Special Olympics athletes, some from states that never see snow . . . and U.S. Olympic silver medalist Billy Kidd with a group of Steamboat Springs' ski instructors. The instructors begin to coach the athletes in the basics of downhill skiing. They expect fear and resistance from these first-time skiers: instead, they find curiosity and a surprising ease on the slopes. By the next day, the athletes ski down a beginner race course, and the first Special Olympics World Winter Games start yet another chapter in the Special Olympics story!

Thanks to those first professional instructors and many others since then, as well as trained volunteer Special Olympics skiing coaches, thousands of Special Olympics athletes around the world enjoy the thrills and the sense of freedom that Alpine skiing can bring. Alpine skiing events include the *downhill*, the *slalom*, and the giant slalom, conducted at the advanced, intermediate, and novice (or beginner) levels. In all of these events, skiers must ski around gates, or flags, as they make their way down the slope. The courses for each event and each level differ in the number of gates used, the vertical drop of the course, and the terrain difficulty. The Unified downhill, giant slalom, and slalom events pair a Special Olympics athlete with a Partner, and their times are combined for a team score.

In 1977, in Steamboat Springs, 500 athletes competed. At the Fifth World Winter Games in 1993 in Schladming and Salzburg, Austria, that number had risen to 1,550. The Games were a dream come true for the athletes as they competed on an internationally known mountain in a country that could be considered the skiing capital of the world! One of those dreams belonged to a joyful young athlete from Lendava, Slovenia, Ignac Levacic, who had worked toward competing in a World Games since joining Special Olympics.

"I was very satisfied with my results in Schladming because I won a silver medal in downhill and a gold medal in the giant slalom. That was my best achievement," Ignac reported. "With my work and training I was helped and encouraged by my best friends. When I returned home they arranged a magnificent reception for me."

The Austrian hills came alive with the sounds of triumph in March 1993.

FRANZ KLAMMER

In February 1976, Patscherkofel Mountain in Innsbruck, Austria was the stage for probably the most awesome Olympic downhill skiing performance of all times. Austrian Franz Klammer waited at the start. Klammer had joined the World Cup circuit in 1972 and had claimed his first World Cup victory in 1973 by breaking the all-time speed record in downhill with an average of 69 miles per hour. Even the "Austrian Astronaut," as Klammer was called, had been stunned by that rocketing trip down the mountain. Between that race and the 1976 Olympic Games, he had kept up his pace and came into the Olympics with a lot to prove as the home-country hero. Bernhard Russi of Switzerland led the downhill as Klammer, the last to race, took off. He flew down the icy slope but at the halfway mark was .19 seconds behind Russi's mid-race time. He finished the race on the tightest line possible, nearly falling into one gate before pulling himself up to whiz to the finish line. He had won—by .33 seconds—and the mountain broke into a sea of ecstatic Austrians!

Special Olympics began in Slovenia, a former republic of Yugoslavia, in 1988. Ignac lives at an institution where people with mental retardation learn and work. He has always enjoyed sports and won a gold medal in the 50-meter dash at Slovenia's first National Special Olympics Games.

His favorite sport is skiing, though. "I spend most of my free time on the snow, because I love speed and love being in nature," Ignac explained. "I like talking about my experiences, my achievements and generally about sports. My colleagues from the national team that went to Austria, we are great friends, even if we live all over Slovenia."

Ignac also enjoys soccer, volleyball, basketball, and cycling, and he does some distance running. As much as sports mean to him, he has a very good way to look at his success. Said Ignac, "Recently I ran in a marathon and had quite a good result, which, of course, is not the most important. All that matters is to participate because it can enrich my life and others'."

Cross-Country Skiing

Cross-country skiing is a way of life that became a sport. In the Scandinavian countries of northern Europe, gliding through the snow on long thin skis is often the best way to get around. (Needless to say, those countries generally dominate Olympic cross-country events!) Athletes in this sport can use the classical technique, sometimes called "kick and glide," keeping their skis in tracks set on the trail before the race, or they can use the free technique, which is like skating, as an athlete pushes off on one ski to glide on the other. Athletes follow a race course marked through the woods, turning with the trail and climbing up hills, then gliding down them.

Special Olympics cross-country athletes compete in races ranging from the 500-meter to the 10-kilometer (or 10k) race, with the 1k, 3k, 5k, and 7.5k in between and the 3x1k relay for teams of three athletes. In all of these except the 5k race, athletes can use free technique. In the 5k race, athletes use classical technique. Unified events include the 1k, 3k, 5k (in which athletes must use classical technique), 7.5k, and 10k races and the 4x1k relay. Unified events combine the best times of a Special Olympics athlete and his or her Partner, while the relay pairs two athletes and two Partners. For athletes of lower ability levels, there are the 50-meter and 100-meter cross-country races and the 10-meter ski race, all using the classical technique, and the glide event.

"When I compete, I feel good and I think how I am going to win. I have won many golden medals in athletics, swimming, basketball, football and cross-country skiing, at many games in Croatia, in Europe, and in America. I intend to be active in sports as long as I can."

—*Zeljko ("Tima") Gasparevic, Croatian Special Olympics athlete*

Most cross-country skiing training programs include dry-land training, or training without snow. This could be working on fitness and leg strength or wearing skis on special surfaces that let the athletes practice skiing motions before working out on snow. Athletes usually get several chances to practice on a cross-country course before their competitions, and then they are on their own!

Until the 500-meter race at a Virginia Special Olympics Winter Games a few years ago, Dallas Santos had competed only in short running races or team sports. In this race, he would be skiing through the woods alone for more than 10 minutes, with nobody there to tell him what to do or cheer for him.

"That long race was a big deal," said Dallas's father Jim, an internationally known track coach. "The way it's set up, the spectators see the start and the finish. So Dallas was on his own, on a snow-covered mountain, for those 10 minutes or so. He had to learn to focus himself on what he had to do. It was a major accomplishment. We were so proud. And training for that event really did help him concentrate better in school."

When Dallas was born in 1974, Jim was deeply involved with coaching world-class track athletes. He was the track and field coach at California State University at Hayward for 14 years, from 1971 to 1984. His women's team won the national title in 1973. His men's team won the national championship in 1977. He coached five women who competed in Olympic Games. He was a U.S. Olympic coach in track and field for the 1980 Olympic Games. And Jim had to accept that his son had mental retardation and some physical disabilities and would never be a star athlete. But when Jim went to see Dallas compete in Special Olympics, he realized that sports would be even more important for his son than for any Olympian.

"Dallas grew up without any playmates," explained Jim. "His sister Kelly was terrific with him, but he still didn't know how to just play. We soon knew that Special Olympics would be his chance to learn about sports, about games. Dallas has come a long way physically since he first started in Special Olympics. It's a big part of his life."

CROSS-COUNTRY STARS

To say that Norwegians love cross-country skiing would be an Olympic-sized understatement! The most popular site at the 1994 Olympic Winter Games in Lillehammer, Norway was the Birkebeineren Ski Stadium, where cross-country races began and ended. The stadium sold out 31,000 seats for each race. Some 100,000 more fans lined the race courses through the woods—many of those fans camping and cooking out for the whole Games! Their spirit paid off: Norwegian Bjorn Dahlie won both the 10k race and the 15k pursuit (which combines the 10k and a 15k race), while Tomas Alsgaard surprised everyone with a victory in the grueling 30k race. Sture Sivertsen added a bronze in the 50k, Marit Wold earned a silver in the women's 15k, and both the men's and women's relay teams raced to silver medals. These athletes brought glory to their country of snow—and those 100,000 fans turned the cold woods into one big celebration!

All of Jim's past experience helps him in his job at Special Olympics International Headquarters in Washington, D.C., USA where he is working to build a worldwide Family Program.

"Special Olympics is the international sports organization most devoted to supporting families in support of the athletes," said Jim. "Raising a child with mental retardation is a challenge, and we create a support system for families so they can see each other and share experiences and ideas."

Figure Skating

Special Olympics figure skating athletes love the beauty and grace of their sport, just as they love to watch well-known skaters such as Brian Boitano, Katarina Witt, Elvis Stojko, and Nancy Kerrigan perform. Athletes compete in singles, pairs, and ice dancing and in Unified pairs and ice dancing. Each event combines scores in compulsories—required elements that are judged for technical correctness—and freestyle, which also includes required elements but allows more artistic expression. Each event is conducted at a number of levels, with different required elements according to ability level.

Athletes who train for figure skating take a series of skill assessment tests through which they earn badges. This badge program, modeled after the United States Figure Skating Association's (USFSA) program for young skaters, marks each athlete's progress so that he or she competes at the best possible level. Many Special Olympics athletes move on to earn more advanced USFSA badges and compete in non–Special Olympics events.

As Nova Scotia, Canada's Julie Stanhope steadily advances in her figure skating skills, she is working hard to pass her success on to other skaters. In this she is following a role model: 1985 World Games skater Sherri Martin, who helped Julie train for the 1989 World Winter Games. Julie set her sights on helping other skaters the way that Sherri had helped her. After winning a gold medal in level 2 skating at the 1989 World Games, the once-shy skater had the confidence to demonstrate skills as coach Mary Ann Crowley taught them.

"Julie's a wonderful example of an athlete who knows that once you attain your goal, you can't stop there," said Mary Ann, a long-time skating coach who was ready for retirement when the request came that she coach Special Olympics athletes. "For someone who passes on their skills to other athletes, their success in sports never ends—that person will always be wanted. Julie is like that." Julie and Sherri now help teach a group of preschool skaters, as well as helping with their close-knit group of ten Special Olympics athletes.

Special Olympics figure skaters work for both technique and artistry.

OKSANA BAIUL

There had never been an Olympic figure skating champion quite like the tearful 16 year old who clung to her coach while the scores flashed their verdict in the women's finals at the 1994 Olympic Winter Games in Lillehammer, Norway. By a margin of one-tenth of one point, Oksana Baiul had won the gold medal! Oksana, who was in second place when the finals began, performed brilliantly in the long program to edge out American Nancy Kerrigan, who had led the field entering that night's competition. Oksana was born in Ukraine, a part of the former Soviet Union. Her father disappeared when she was two, and her mother died of cancer when Oksana was 13. Oksana was already a successful skater, and she made up her mind to continue skating. In 1992 she moved to the city of Odessa to live and train with Galina Zmievskaya, who also coached Viktor Petrenko, the 1992 Olympic gold medalist in men's figure skating. With the help and friendship of Galina and Viktor, Oksana quickly proved her abilities on the world stage with a win at the 1993 World Championship. From there, she headed straight for Olympic gold!

Julie competed in level 3 skating at the 1993 World Winter Games and brought home a hard-won bronze medal. Two years ago she was invited to a skating demonstration with, among others, Canadian Olympic star Brian Orser. Julie and others had a chance to improvise a routine for the crowd. According to Mary Ann, Julie stood out among all of the skaters for her artistic impression.

"One of Julie's strengths is the way she feels the music," said Mary Ann. "She loves music and it shows—her level of expression is beyond any of us. She's just uninhibited when it comes to skating!" Julie likes mixing moods and rhythms in her routines, showing equal skill with slow and fast pieces. Perhaps her favorite tune says it all for such a performing artist as Julie Stanhope: "There's No Business Like Show Business!"

Canada's Julie Stanhope (left) loved the excitement of the 1993 World Games.

Speed Skating

From the grace of the figure skaters, we'll move on to the sport of speed skating. These athletes are graceful too—after all, they have to stay on their feet as they speed around an ice rink. Like cross-country skiers, good speed skaters train to find a rhythm in their arms and legs to help them move as quickly and efficiently as possible. In longer events, that rhythm helps them not waste their strength or energy. A successful speed skater is quick at the start, sprinting out to try and take the lead around the inside of the track to force the other racers to pass on the outside. After that it's a matter of concentration—thinking only of pushing forward and not of who's behind you or beside you!

Individual events in speed skating are the 100-meter, 300m, 500m, 800m, 1,000m, and 1,500m races. Three Unified relays and a sprint event provide competition for teams. In the 1,500-meter Unified relay, two athletes and two Partners each skate at least three laps, with the last two (of 15, on a ice hockey–size rink) completed by an athlete. The fastest combined time wins each division. In the 4x400m Unified relay, the two athletes and two Partners each skate 400 meters, with hand tag or push starts between team members, just like in the 1,500m relay. The third relay is the 4x500m, 4,000m Unified relay, in which the athletes and Partners each skate 500 meters twice. In the final event, one athlete and one Partner each skate both a 500m and a 1,000m race their times are added and averaged for the final score.

Tracy Jennings began skating with a *therapeutic* ice skating program in her home town of Old Bridge, New Jersey, USA when she was eight. She joined a Special Olympics speed skating training program in December 1991. Her natural athletic talent and endurance enabled her to win a gold and silver medal just a few months later in the 1992 New Jersey Winter Special Olympics Games.

A young athlete ready for the start of a speed skating race!

BONNIE BLAIR

Bonnie Blair grew up in Champaign, Illinois, USA. She was the youngest of six children in a close-knit family. As a child, she had to hustle to keep up with her older brothers and sisters—to be "one of the gang." Luckily, the gang loved skating and by the time Bonnie was four, she was racing! With her family behind her every step of the way, Bonnie has raced her way into the record books. She won her first gold medal at the 1988 Winter Olympic Games in Calgary, Canada in the 500m. She then went on to win both the 500m and 1,000m in 1992 at the Winter Olympics in Albertville, France. At the 1994 Olympic Winter Games in Lillehammer, Norway, the gold medals she earned in the 500m and 1,000m speed skating events brought her Olympic total to five golds—the most that any American woman has won. Bonnie's latest achievement was breaking the 39-second barrier in the women's 500m. Her time of 38:99 at a Calgary invitational just after the 1994 Winter Olympics compares to the famous runner Roger Bannister breaking the four-minute mile in 1954! Bonnie retired in 1995, still in peak form but ready to move on in life.

As a gold medal winner, Tracy was one of the thousands of American Special Olympics gold medal speed skaters with a chance to compete in the 1993 World Winter Games in Austria as members of Team USA. Tracy's name was one of those chosen at random for the team! At first, Tracy was nervous about traveling so far away from home with so many new people. But when her training began in earnest in December of 1992 at the Team USA speed skating training camp in Lake Placid, New York, Tracy's competitiveness and drive overcame her fears.

After winning two more gold medals at the 1993 New Jersey State Games that February, Tracy was ready for Austria. Her town raised the money to send her family to the World Games. One money-maker was a good luck banner that people paid five dollars each to sign. Tracy's parents and younger brother took it to Austria and held it up for her in the stands!

When Tracy returned to Old Bridge with two silver medals in the 100m and 300m speed skating events, the town was

Olympic gold medalist Dan Jansen (right) left his skates behind to attend the 1995 World Games.

thrilled. She had become a local hero. There were newspaper articles about her and a special reception on "Tracy Jennings Day," when the mayor presented her with a plaque and spoke of the town's pride in her.

Chapter 7

The Special Olympics summer events give athletes a chance to compete in widely popular sports such as track and soccer and also in fun lifetime sports like bowling and tennis.

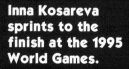

Inna Kosareva sprints to the finish at the 1995 World Games.

Sprint, Swim, and Split

Aquatics

Special Olympics swimming dates back to the very beginning, back to Eunice Kennedy Shriver's camp in Maryland in the early 1960s. The first Special Olympics Games in 1968 featured an above-ground pool on the grass of Chicago's Soldier Field. Dozens of volunteers stood along the edge of the pool, ready to save any athletes in trouble. But the swimmers swam true to their training and no rescues were needed!

Official swimming events include: freestyle (50-meter, 100m, 200m, 400m, 800m, and 1,500m), backstroke (50m, 100m, and 200m), breaststroke (50m, 100m, and 200m), butterfly (50m, 100m, and 200m), individual medley (100m, 200m, and 400m), freestyle relays (4x25m, 4x50m, and 4x100m), and medley relays (4x25m, 4x50m, and 4x100m). Shorter events in swimming, walking, and flotation provide competition for athletes with lower abilities.

Divers compete in the one-meter springboard event, performing dives defined by the Federation Internationale de Natacion Amateur (FINA), or International Amateur Swimming Federation.

Aquatics athletes usually train all spring for their local, chapter, or national Summer Games. They practice all of the strokes, then swim their best stroke in competition. The recent addition of difficult events such as the 800m and 1,500m

At the 1956 Olympic Games in Melbourne, Australian Dawn Fraser broke the world record in her preliminary heat of the 100-meter freestyle event, then broke it again to win the gold medal in 1:02.00! Dawn also placed second in the 400-meter freestyle and helped Australia to a gold-medal finish in

DAWN FRASER

the 4x100-meter relay. Dawn competed in the 1960 and 1964 Olympic Games, winning the 100-meter freestyle in both. In 1962, she became the first woman to swim 100 meters in under a minute. In 1964, she swam her best time of 58.9 seconds in that event, setting a record that stood until 1971.

freestyle and the 400m individual medley show how excellent training and better fitness habits have greatly improved the abilities of Special Olympics athletes.

Kamala Gesteland's training schedule would be right up there with an Olympic athlete's. For years now, this tiny spitfire has run five miles and swum 3,000 meters each day. The training paid off: At the 1995 World Summer Games, Kamala won bronze medals in the top divisions of the 200m and 400m freestyle, a gold medal in the 100m individual medley, and two gold medals in the 200m and 400m freestyle relays.

If training for the 1995 World Games was a challenge, it was one that Kamala faced joyfully after the challenges of her early life. She spent her first years at the

Some 600 swimmers showed their skills in the 50-meter pool at the 1995 World Games.

Mother Teresa Home for the Destitute and Dying, an orphanage in New Delhi, India, unable to speak, chew, or swallow. From there she was sent to a home for the "hopelessly handicapped," where she was expected to die from her disabilities.

Months of training pay off for this coach and athlete.

But miraculously, things turned around. A physical therapist at the home began to work with her, and Kamala learned to walk, ride a tricycle, and speak a few words. Then an American volunteer named Hopi Gesteland took an interest in her. She brought Kamala home for a visit, and Hopi's husband and four sons fell in love with her. When it was time for them to leave India, the boys refused to leave without her—so they adopted Kamala.

After living in Italy, Germany, and Singapore—where Kamala began her rigorous daily training schedule as part of the "Fighting Fish" swim team—the Gestelands returned to Wisconsin, USA in 1993. That was when Kamala plunged into Special Olympics sports. According to Kamala's mother, the 1995 World Games were a turning point in Kamala's life. "She loved the Games—loved going to the athlete dances, loved eating a lot, loved watching other athletes swim," said Hopi. "She seemed to become more outgoing while she was in Connecticut, and has been trying out this new independence since we've been back!"

Long jumpers have three attempts to score their best jumps.

Athletics

More Special Olympics athletes around the world participate in athletics, or track and field, than in any other sport. For one reason, there are more events to appeal to athletes and match their strengths. For another reason, most events require no special equipment or facilities for training and even competition. Because track and field events use basic physical skills such as walking, running, throwing, and jumping, they often serve as a starting point for athletes who can master both the physical skills and the competition techniques.

Running events include: the 100-meter, 200m, and 400m dash; the 800m run; the 100m hurdles for women; the 110m hurdles for men; and the 4x100m and 4x400m relay. Race walking events are the 100m, 400m, and 800m walk. Long

distance events include: the 1,500m, 3,000m, 5,000m, and 10,000m, held as both runs and walks; the 15,000 walk; the half marathon (13.5 miles) and the marathon (26.2 miles).

Field events range from the high jump, long jump, and shot put (with shots of various weights depending on the age and gender of the athletes) to the pentathlon, in which the athlete's score is based on results in five events: the 100m dash, long jump, shot put, high jump, and 400m run.

Athletes using wheelchairs can compete in the 100m, 200m, and 400m race and wheelchair shot put. For athletes with lower ability levels, the sport offers shorter walks and wheelchair races, assisted walks, softball throw, standing long jump, and wheelchair relay, motorized wheelchair slalom and obstacle course, and (tennis) ball throw.

Above: Success in the shot put depends on upper body strength. Right: As these runners show, relays demand individual excellence—and teamwork.

A visit to the track at the 1995 World Summer Games showed the amazing range of abilities and backgrounds of Special Olympics athletes. Three speedsters finished their division of the men's 100m dash within .22 seconds of each other—with the winning time at 11.77 seconds. Wheelchair athletes pushed their arms to the limit in their 400m race. The top women's high jump was 1.25 meters (4.16 feet), a height reached by three athletes.

Meanwhile, the USA's Holly Mandy won the 3,000m run in 12:00 and the 1,500m run in 5:39, and she earned a silver in the half marathon, finishing in one hour and 55 minutes. According to her mother, "Holly ran like a house on fire. In all her years of running, she just couldn't break either a 13-minute 3,000, or a six-minute 1,500—and she did both at the World Games!"

TRACK LEGENDS

On the long list of Olympic track legends, three stand out for their determination to overcome a severe obstacle. Harold Connolly was born with a left arm crippled from nerve damage but won the 1956 gold medal in the hammer throw. He went on to compete in the 1960, 1964, and 1968 Olympic Games; held the world record seven times; and represented the United States in 66 international competitions. Wilma Rudolph won three gold medals for the USA at the 1960 Olympic Games: in the 200m (becoming the first woman to break 23 seconds); the 100m dash (by three yards—with a sprained ankle!); and the 4 x 100m relay. From age four to 12, Wilma had worn steel braces and special shoes because of a crippling attack of scarlet fever. By age 16, this amazing athlete competed in track in the 1956 Olympic Games in Melbourne, Australia, winning a bronze medal in the 4x100m relay on the way to her triumph in Rome! Gail Devers, an American sprinter, began suffering from Graves' disease (which affects the thyroid, a gland that regulates growth and hormones) in 1988. Radiation therapy caused her feet to swell so much that doctors considered amputating them. Just in time, they realized that the radiation was to blame and changed her treatment. In an amazing turn of events, those feet led Gail right back to track stardom and to a gold medal in the 100m dash at the 1992 Summer Olympic Games!

Holly Mandy ran personal-best times in her events at the 1995 World Games.

This was Holly's second trip to the World Games: she had earned a silver medal in the 5,000m run at the 1991 Special Olympics World Summer Games with a time of 24:44.8 seconds, just a fraction of a second behind the winner. That fraction of a second motivated her to train harder than ever so that she'd never be edged out again. Sure enough, throughout the 1,500m race at the 1995 World Games, she traded the lead with a runner from Panama until, going into the bell lap, she pulled away and won.

Holly comes from an athletic family, and she loves to run. She decided to join her high school cross-country team in Clinton township, Michigan, even though her teammates weren't thrilled about the "special ed kid" running with them. Then they saw her race, and they began to believe in her. By the time an important race came at the end of the season, they were cheering her on to the finish that would earn her a varsity letter.

Holly earned eight varsity letters during her high school career (four in cross-country and four in track). In 1992, she was one of the 21 runners named to the

"...it shows me what I can do with hard work."

—Holly Mandy,
Special Olympics athlete

all-county cross-country team and ran in the Michigan State Finals in cross-country. As the first special education student in her school district to earn a varsity letter, Holly made believers of a lot of people.

"Sports lets me be proud of who I am and what I can do," says Holly, who has competed in Special Olympics since age ten, training in track, bowling, football (soccer)*, basketball, swimming, and cross-country skiing. "I also like sports because of meeting friends. Running helps keep me in shape and keeps me from watching TV all day. I know it makes me be responsible and that will help me for when I do have a job. Plus it shows me what I can do with hard work."

And she does work hard! To prepare for her three races at the Games, Holly ran 10 to 12 miles five times a week, lifted weights every night, and did speed work once a week with a local roadrunners club. Holly gets a lot of support from her family—especially because her 15-year-old brother Joshua also runs in Special Olympics (he competed in three races at the Games too) and her 13-year-old brother Drew competes in assisted swim events.

Bowling

Athletes who compete in Special Olympics bowling love raising the eyebrows of friends as well as strangers who are surprised at their skill and high scores. Bowling attracts many athletes because it is such a social sport, and one that they can participate in with friends and family all their lives. A sign of the sports' growing popularity is the increase in the number of athletes competing in bowling at World Games: 33 athletes, mostly from the United States, competed in 1987, and 454 athletes from 23 countries competed in 1995!

Competition events in bowling include standard singles; ramp unassisted and assisted bowl for athletes with physical disabilities; male, female, and mixed doubles; and male, female, and mixed teams (of four athletes). Unified Bowling matches athletes with and without mental retardation in doubles and team events. Athletes of lower ability levels compete in target bowl and frame bowl.

Bowling is a super sport for athletes with physical disabilities.

* What people in the United States know as *soccer* is called *football* throughout most of the rest of the world. In Special Olympics, it is called *football*.

A N   O L Y M P I C   P R O F I L E

BOWLING

While bowling is not an Olympic sport, it holds a unique spot at Olympic Games. The 1988 Summer Olympics in Seoul, Korea did include bowling as an exhibition sport. The two bowlers representing the United States were Mark Lewis—who has gone on to coach the United Arab Emirates national team—and Debbie McMullen, now a mem- ber of the professional tour. In Barcelona in 1992, Olympic athletes were treated to a bowling center in Olympic Village. For the 1996 Olympic Games in Atlanta, top ama- teurs will compete just before the Games open, then stay around to give demonstra- tions for Olympic athletes, who will have a chance to bowl as well.

"...Special Olympics is more even than sports. It helps me respect others and get respect back."

—Loretta Claiborne,
Special Olympics athlete

One of the bowling stars at the 1995 World Games has made her mark in other Special Olympics sports as well. Loretta Claiborne bowled a personal best 178 on the way to a gold medal in the top singles division, and teamed up for another gold in mixed teams. Talk about lifting eyebrows! Loretta was born in 1953 with mental retardation and problems with her feet and her eyes.

Doctors told her mother that Loretta should be put in an institution. They said she would not walk until very late, would probably never run, and would not get beyond fourth grade.

With a high school diploma, countless Special Olympics medals and ribbons, awards from sports organizations, and an honorary doctorate degree tucked under her black belt in karate, Loretta has proven those predictions wrong!

"After the World Games, I wanted to defect—back to the dorms and all of the great athletes there," said Loretta Claiborne.

A native of York, Pennsylvania, USA, Loretta began running at the age of 13 with her older brother Hank. At that time, she could not participate in school sports because she was a special education stu- dent. Three years later, someone suggested that she try Special Olympics. She began competing that year and in 1972 traveled to Los Angeles, California to compete in track at the Third Special Olympics World Summer Games.

In 1983, Loretta won the mile run in 5:45 at the Fifth World Summer Games. She was the top woman finisher in the half marathon at the 1991 World Games and placed second in her division of the 5,000-meters, running the two races just one day apart! Over the years, Loretta has also competed in Special Olympics basketball, Alpine skiing, figure skating, roller-skating, football (soccer), and volleyball.

Loretta's most important sports accomplishment may be outside of Special Olympics. She has run in more than 26 marathons, clocking her best time of 3:03 at the 1982 Boston Marathon. She knows that running against "normal" athletes helps build understanding about the abilities of people with mental retardation. Loretta was one of the first Special Olympics athletes to run marathons; now hundreds compete in marathons around the world.

"When I was little I had a very tough time in school, but when it came to playing sports I could excel," said Loretta. "Sports was and still is an outlet for me. It also keeps me physically fit and that helps my overall health, like heart rate and blood pressure. And Special Olympics is more even than sports. It helps me respect others and get respect back. And most of all it has helped me to get over so many hurdles and to say to myself, 'I am who I am, but I can be the best of who I am'."

Loretta keeps a busy schedule of training, volunteering, and public speaking. The only athlete member of the Board of Directors of Special Olympics International, Loretta helped find sponsors and train volunteers for the 1995 World Games. In 1991, *Runner's World* magazine honored Loretta as the greatest Special Olympics runner of the quarter century. And in 1993, she was inducted into the National Girls and Women in Sport Symposium Hall of Fame.

Cycling

Cycling became an official Special Olympics sport in 1988, after several years as a demonstration sport. Competition events are: 500-meter, 1-kilometer, 5k, and 10k time trials; and the 5k, 10k, 15k, 25k, and 40k road races. In a time trial, athletes are started along a course at 30-second or one-minute intervals, and the winner is determined by the fastest time. In a road race, athletes start together and the first front tire to cross the finish line determines the winner.

Conrad DuPreez of South Africa saw his tire cross first in two of the exciting road races at the 1995 World Games.

Conrad DuPreez (third from left) brought home three medals to South Africa.

Special Olympics cyclists take over the streets when the Games are in town.

AN OLYMPIC PROFILE

CYCLING SUPER-STARS

Many Olympic speed skating stars turn their awesome leg strength into success by cycling. Here are two that stand out. Sheila Young of the U.S. won a gold, silver, and bronze medal at the 1976 Olympic Winter Games and held the world and Olympic records in the 500-meters. During and after her spectacular skating career, she won world cycling championships in 1973, 1976, and 1981. Eric Heiden won five speed skating events at the 1980 Olympics Games: the 500m and 1,000m sprint events, the 1,500m and 5,000m middle distance events, and the long-distance 10,000m. In all five he broke Olympic records—and one world record. No other athlete before or since has won five individual gold medals in a single Olympic Games. (American swimmer Mark Spitz won seven gold medals in 1972, but three were for relays). Eric kept his awesome Olympic performance in perspective. He retired from speed skating right after the 1980 Games and entered medical school to become an orthopedic surgeon. Eric won a U.S. professional cycling championship in 1985, but after racing in the 1986 Tour de France he was right back to the operating room!

Conrad raced to gold in the 15k race with time of 24:13, and in the "marathon" 40k, in 1.03. These times topped previous Special Olympics bests and earned Conrad instant fame in his country.

Before seven years ago, Conrad had never raced. He had bought a motorbike and was out in front of his house working on the engine when a group of cyclists rode by. The sport caught his fancy, and he immediately traded in his motorbike for a racing cycle. He loves to ride, training for 17 kilometers (around 10 miles) in the morning before work, and 60k (36 miles) when he gets home in the evening. He also adds to his racing expertise as a member of the BMW Power Wheelers Club in his home city of Pretoria, and by attending professional cycling races and watching the pros.

South Africa officially joined the Special Olympics movement in 1992, and the program is growing fast. It's one of many changes rocketing through the country. For most of its history, the country had been ruled by apartheid laws, which separated white and black people and gave the native black people no rights to vote. Those laws have finally been abolished and a free election has been held. In 1992, South Africa also officially returned to the Olympic Games after being banned from the Games for 32 years because of apartheid.

Paul Mogotsi, a black South African cycling coach, sees the South African delegation to the 1995 World Games as a symbol of changes sweeping the country, as black and white Special Olympics athletes and coaches train, travel, and compete together. "These athletes are very prepared, ready and excited," Paul said before the Games, "and I look forward to the changes that Special Olympics and our athletes will bring home to South Africa."

Equestrian Sports

Few sports give a Special Olympics athlete the leap of confidence that comes with equestrian sports. Imagine the feeling of guiding and controlling a big, beautiful horse—and winning a medal for your poise and precision! Equestrian sports became an official Special Olympics sport in 1988 after its years as a demonstration sport had shown how valuable it would be for athletes.

Events represent both English and Western riding techniques, and include: *dressage*; English *equitation* on the flat; stock seat equitation; working trails; the rodeo events of pole bending and barrel racing; drill teams of twos or fours; *prix caprilli* (jumps); *showmanship* at halter/bridle; and team relays.

While the skill of the riders is important, the horses' abilities contribute as much, or more, to the final outcome! One equestrian athlete at the 1995 World Games who worried about not competing with his own mount was Chad Kocabinski of South Dakota, USA. Chad had been riding for years, always with a special Palamino named Casey. He couldn't bring Casey to the 1995 World Games, but good quality quarter horses from around New England were brought in and matched to athletes by size and temperament. With more than 350 athletes of all ability levels coming from 33 countries—including South Africa, Guadeloupe, Russia, and the Isle of Man—this was no easy task!

Left: Chad Kocabinski made the most of his new mount at 1995 World Games. Below: Special Olympics equestrian athlete jumps English style.

Chad's new mount was named Can Bea Scotch, and they had only three days to become a team. "She was really smooth and gentle," Chad said of Scotch. The same can be said of Chad: the six-foot, nine-inch tall athlete is often called a "gentle giant" for his manners and laid-back approach to life. Chad and Scotch teamed up to win a gold medal in stock seat equitation and a bronze medal in showmanship at halter.

Chad's family had traveled from South Dakota to watch him compete. With tears streaming down his face, Chad's father stood and watched his son receive his gold medal. "I wanted to jump up and down," said Mike

Special Olympics equestrian sports include both English and Western events. These two styles differ in the kind of tack (reins, bridles, and saddles) used and in the way a rider sits and rides. Dressage is an English event in which a horse and rider go through a set pattern of walking, trotting, and cantering and are judged by how precisely and fluidly they move together through these steps. The prix caprilli event (also English) adds jumps into the dressage pattern. In the equitation event (English and stock seat, or Western), riders compete as a class (or group) by moving through a walk and trot as they proceed around the ring. This event is usually for lower ability level athletes who may be assisted by a volunteer leader and sidewalker. Showmanship (with halter for Western and bridle for English) requires a standing athlete to "show" his or her horse to a judge by moving from standing to walking and turning while the judge inspects it. The Western event of working trails tests an athlete on situations he or she would encounter on an actual trail, such as walking the horse through a gate, over a bridge, and through a zig-zag pattern of poles. In the Western event of pole bending, the athlete and horse are timed on weaving through six poles. A barrel race, also Western, takes the horse and rider around a barrel and back to the start. Drill teams perform routines to music while riding.

Kocabinski. "It was wild. I don't know when I've experienced anything like this. It's just a wonderful, wonderful thing."

Remember those "experts" who had said that people with mental retardation couldn't learn sports? Picture the parents of those children, told not to encourage regular physical activity in their children . . . and picture Mike Kocabinski, thrilled to tears as his son stands high on a Special Olympics award stand to be honored for athletic success!

Gymnastics

Enter a Special Olympics gymnastics competition, and you enter a world of intense concentration, supple strength, and dreams of glory. Like their Olympic counterparts, all Special Olympics gymnasts work hard to train their bodies to stretch and jump and balance. Female artistic gymnasts compete in vaulting, uneven bars, balance beam, floor exercise, and the all-around, which combines scores in each event. Male gymnasts compete in floor exercise, pommel horse, rings, vaulting, parallel bars, horizontal bar, and all-around. Athletes in these events compete at different levels according to their abilities. Level A events for athletes of lower ability levels are wide beam, tumbling, floor exercise, and vaulting.

Rhythmic gymnasts do not use artistic *apparatus*, but they do use a rope, hoop, ball, and ribbon for dance-type routines set to music. The all-around combines scores in each of these events. Female gymnasts can also do group routines with the hoop, ball, or ribbon.

Special Olympics gymnasts can inspire with their skill—or their determination. At the 1987 World Games in South Bend, Indiana, USA, the capacity crowd held its breath as Philip Schmuck of Nevada, USA performed his routine on the pommel horse. Philip has cerebral palsy, a birth defect that affects muscle coordination

Philip Schmuck concentrates on his pommel horse routine.

and speech. He is also deaf. Though extremely strong, the 34-year-old athlete had to use every bit of his strength and concentration to move arms and legs with amazing precision through the routine. Philip's strength triumphed—he won six gold medals in his division at the Games.

In the category of pure skill, there is Robert Vasquez. The twelve-year-old from Virginia, USA competed in the top level of gymnastics at the 1995 World Games. In his best event, the rings, Bobby earned a gold medal. Bobby also won four silvers: in the floor exercise, vault, pommel horse, and all-around; one bronze, in the parallel bars; and a fourth place in the high bars.

Bobby's coach Shane Revill, who also coaches non–Special Olympics athletes, considers Bobby's skill and his flexibility in a league with many regular gymnasts. The biggest obstacle to Bobby's success is his frustration when he can't do a move or when things don't go his way. "We had trouble on the first day of competition, when we got a score we didn't agree with," said Shane. "I thought Bobby would be down for the rest of the week. But the next day, he went on his own and apologized to the official for his poor

AN OLYMPIC PROFILE

In 1975, Nadia Comaneci became the youngest gymnast ever to win the European championship. She was only 13 years old. A year later, she stunned the world with the difficulty of her routines at the Montreal Olympic Games. She received seven perfect 10 scores for her performance—no one in Olympic gymnastics history had earned even one 10! Nadia won gold medals in the all-around competition, uneven bars, and

NADIA COMANECI

balance beam; a bronze in the floor exercise; and a silver in the team competition. The young gymnast returned to the Olympic Games in 1980. She won the silver in the all-around after a controversial score by the judges from the U.S.S.R. and Poland put a Soviet gymnast in first place. Nadia retired from the sport in 1984 and in 1989 came to America to escape the hard life of communist Romania.

sportsmanship. Then the group he was competing with came together, almost like a team, instead of athletes competing against each other. High fives, great attitudes—it ended up being the meet of everyone's lives! Bobby ate it up and did a flawless routine on the rings to win the gold."

Roller-Skating

As a relatively new official sport, roller-skating may not have the biggest number of athletes around the world—but what it lacks in numbers, it makes up for in intensity! Athletes who compete in roller-skating love the sport and love to watch it. Fans at the

roller-skating events at the 1995 World Games went crazy for their athletes, and the athletes performed beyond expectations.

Speed events include the 100-meter, 300m, 500m, and 1,000m races and the 2 x 100m, 2 x 200m, and 4 x 100m relays. Athletes of lower ability levels compete in the 30m straight line race and the 30m slalom. Artistic skaters compete in school figures, freestyle singles, freestyle pairs, and solo and team dance. As with gymnastics and figure skating, artistic roller-skating has four levels for athletes to compete in, with different required elements for each level.

Roller hockey is played with five players to a team, each using a smaller stick than the sticks used for ice hockey. Players can choose either in-line or quad skates, just as they can for the

Costumes and music help artistic roller skaters put on a good show.

A N   O L Y M P I C   P R O F I L E

OLYMPIC COACH

One of the celebrity medal presenters at the 1995 World Games roller-skating events was Yale University ice hockey coach Tim Taylor. He stood and watched the freestyle singles competition and spoke about this first experience at Special Olympics. "It's more of an honor for me to meet them than for them to meet me," said Taylor, who was the head coach of the U.S. hockey team at the 1994 Olympic Games. "When we fin- ished eighth at the Winter '94 Olympics— the worse U.S. finish ever—I don't think my athletes handled it so well. Even though all Olympic athletes don't expect to win gold, I think we did—our goals were tied to a medal. These Special Olympics athletes keep things in perspective—they think in terms of personal bests, of just being here. Handing out awards to them has been a true Olympic experience."

other events. In-line skates are usually faster but are also tougher to control, so athletes decide based on their own strengths.

The award for the loudest cheering section at the 1995 World Games roller-skating events would definitely go to Argentina. (Roller-skating is very popular in that country, and its athletes lead the world at international events.) When Gabriel Salas, age 21, won his division of the 500m race, some 20 Argentinians cheered, chanted, sang, and hugged throughout the whole medal ceremony. Gabriel also won a bronze in the 300m, but it was the gold that he won "for his mother and father."

Gabriel lives at home and goes to school—and practices his skating for at least an hour a day. "He doesn't need pushing," said Gabriel's father Hector. "Because he doesn't hear or speak it is better for his conditioning because he concentrates. He is a great athlete and loves this team."

An hour later, Gabriel and artistic skater Eugenia Guidi did their best to comfort teammate Martin D'Andrea, who placed second in his division of freestyle singles. With the support of his friends, Martin realized that the Argentinian fans didn't expect all gold medals!

Above: Gabriel Salas, shown here with his father, won his gold medal "for his parents" at the 1995 World Games. Below: A player prepares to serve at the 1995 World Games tennis venue.

Tennis

The crowd hushes for the serve . . . the serve is good . . . the return goes down the line for a point! Special Olympics tennis athletes compete with intensity, but also with true enjoyment of the lifelong sport. Events include singles and doubles (played to one six-game set, with a nine-point tie-breaker if necessary), and the individual skills contest to test all of a player's basic tennis skills. Athletes of lower ability levels have the target serve, target bounce, racket bounce, and return shot.

Tennis athletes and coaches around the world have had the privilege of working with top female professional players as part of the Women's Tennis Association's (WTA)

support for Special Olympics. Stars like Steffi Graf, Monica Seles, Gabriela Sabatini, and Aranxta Sanchez Vicario lead the list of players who have shared their skills during tournaments in the United States, Australia, and Europe.

One of the leaders in the sport of tennis at the 1995 World Games was Wisconsin, USA's Cindy Bentley, who won a silver medal in singles and sixth place in doubles. She went home and added them to her Special Olympics collection—a collection that began in 1968. Cindy competed in the very first Special Olympics Games at Chicago's Soldier Field. Since then she has won medals in basketball, track, speed skating, volleyball, and tennis and has also trained in softball and swimming.

Cindy's sense of humor and instinct for being a leader have made her a favorite among Wisconsin's Special Olympics athletes. Her independent and happy life now is a big change from her childhood. She was born with *fetal alcohol syndrome* and an addiction to drugs, through her mother. After a hospital stay to end the addiction, Cindy lived with a few different foster families who didn't treat her very well. Her luck changed when she was moved to a home for people with mental retardation. That's where she started out in Special Olympics. Cindy now lives on her own and works at a McDonalds, training in sports in her time off and giving speeches to groups about Special Olympics!

Top: Tennis star Monica Seles gave coaching pointers to athletes at the 1995 World Games. Bottom: Cindy Bentley (in blue shirt) adds another medal to her 27-year-old collection.

Chapter 8

Team sports add a unique dimension to Special Olympics competition and are played in both summer and winter.

The team from Puerto Rico takes its opponent to the hoop.

Putting It All Together: The Team Sports

Team sports hold an important place in Special Olympics. While players learn the athletic skills needed for the sport, they also learn teamwork and cooperation, and they have the chance to polish important social skills. Special Olympics athletes who play on teams together may develop lifelong friendships. And since the introduction of Unified Sports®, those friendships often form between athletes with and without mental retardation.

A typical eight-week training session for a team sport begins with the basics, as coaches instruct and drill the athletes on the individual skills that go into the sport. For example, in basketball they would work on dribbling and shooting; in softball, throwing and hitting; in football (soccer), kicking, heading, and throw-ins. As the weeks progress, work on team skills such as passing and defense, as well as practice games, help prepare the team for competition. Then the athletes are ready to put all of these skills together and compete as a team. A number of Special Olympics teams train and compete together for many years each time their sport is in season, or move together through different sport seasons.

The same process of putting Special Olympics athletes into divisions for competition happens for teams as well as for individuals. During the training sessions, each athlete on a team takes a skills test, then the players' scores in this test are averaged together to help place the team in the right competition division for the Games or tournament. Team sports also offer individual and team events for athletes with lower ability levels who are not yet ready for full-field play. These events help train and motivate athletes to work hard at improving.

Basketball

Special Olympics athletes can compete in five-on-five basketball or, if their team skills are still developing, in three-on-three half-court basketball. Skills contests for lower-ability athletes include target passing, speed dribbling, and spot shots.

Basketball was an early success of the ground-breaking Unified Sports® program, enabling Special Olympics athletes to play alongside athletes without mental retardation in school and community programs around the world. Unified Partner Dustin Mellott of Evansville, Indiana, USA can speak for this success. "I was thrilled when I made our school's Unified Basketball team," said Dustin. "I see my teammates as normal, not as individuals with a disability. Playing for the team improved not only my basketball skills, but also my sportsmanship—we were told to really encourage the Special Olympics athletes, but it ended up being both ways—they cheered me on, too!"

Dustin's sports heroes are the 1992 U.S. Olympic Basketball Dream Team and track star Carl Lewis. "I think any Olympic athlete would have been a part of a Unified Sports® team if it was around when they were in school," Dustin said.

Like Dustin, Special Olympics athlete Mark Swiconek of Plainville, Connecticut, USA loves to talk about Special Olympics—and about basketball. And does he talk! A Toastmaster for many years, Mark was among the first Athletes for Outreach trained to speak to groups—from potential athletes, to civic clubs, to teacher conferences—about Special Olympics. One of his treasured memories is introducing Eunice Kennedy Shriver, the founder of Special Olympics, to the crowd of 60,000 people at the Opening Ceremonies of the 1991 World Games. Mark served on the board

The team from Kazakhstan traveled through ten time zones to compete in New Haven.

AN OLYMPIC PROFILE

THE DREAM TEAM

It was every basketball fan's dream of a team. The 1992 U.S. men's Olympic basketball team brought together the athletic brilliance of Michael Jordan, Larry Bird, Magic Johnson, Scottie Pippen, Chris Mullin, Charles Barkley, Karl Malone, Clyde Drexler, Patric Ewing, David Robinson, John Stockton, and Christian Laettner. No one doubted that the Dream Team would win the gold medal in Barcelona—it was just a question of by how much. The U.S. defeated eight opponents by an average of 43.8 points, with a final win of 117–85 over a tenacious team from war-torn Croatia. This first trip by professional players to the Olympics (the rules were changed in 1988) was almost certainly the best that will ever be.

of directors for the 1995 World Games and broke new ground as a reporter for New Haven's CBS-TV station.

As far as competing, Mark's done a little of everything. "I began competing in Special Olympics in 1973," says Mark. "I was 15 at the time. Since then I have won medals in running and walking events, the standing long jump, basketball, and bowling. I have also competed in softball.

"My favorite sport is basketball, because it's the one I really excel in and it's the sport that pushes me to my limit. My best game was when I scored 42 points in the gold medal game at our State Games in 1993. Right now I train seven days a week. Monday to Friday at lunchtime in the fitness room at Stanley Works, where I work. Thursday nights are basketball or softball practice, depending on the season. Friday through Monday nights, I bowl.

Mark Swiconek earned his biggest honor in 1995: the Spirit of Special Olympics Award.

"When I'm competing, I get a great feeling of accomplishment, and I also know I've improved my health. There is one other thing I would like to tell people reading this. Go out to a Special Olympics event and see for yourselves what people with mental retardation can do when given a fair chance!"

Football (Soccer)

Football's popularity leads the Special Olympics team sports—as it leads team sports around the world. At the 1995 World Games, more than 1,000 athletes from 67 countries represented the estimated 150,000 athletes worldwide who train and compete in football. Special Olympics football athletes consider the World Games their own

World Cup, and they love to play for their countries in tough match-ups.
Traditional powers at World Games are Chile, Germany, and Ireland, as athletes
from those countries play from the time they are very young!

Special Olympics football competition includes 11-a-side games; 5-a-side games
on smaller fields, with smaller goals; and Unified games of both size teams. The
individual skills contest for athletes of lower ability levels includes dribbling, shooting, and run and kick.

The football competition at the 1995 World Games held non-stop highlights.
At the upper skill level, the expert team from Chile was unseated as champions of
the top division after holding that spot for the last two World Games. After romp-
ing through the preliminary rounds of the tournament, speedy Chile lost its luck
in the gold-medal game, with shots banging off the goalposts and goalkeeper. A
strong, well-coached German team pulled off the 2–1 upset.

On the 5-a-side fields, a goal by 24-year-old Jesus Marin helped lead Spain to a 3–1 win over Jamaica—and Jesus in turn led his team and their fans in chanting "España, España" ("Spain, Spain") as he embraced every player. On the next field, Firman Young was everywhere on defense for his team from Nova Scotia, Canada, with 13-year Special Olympics veteran Kenneth Moser a willing substitute when Firman needed a break.

The Connecticut Unified five-a-side team stands out for the super performances turned in by the Special Olympics athletes on the team and the team's tremendous unity. Of the team's six games, a Partner scored in only one—all of the rest of the goals were scored by athletes with mental retardation. Athlete Raul Ramos, who shined in goal, worked at his skills every day to prepare for the Games. "I eat, sleep and dream soccer," said Raul. "It gives me a reason to be on earth."

The whole team shared Raul's passion for the sport. Every player was out there because he loved the game—and that love helped overcome the disappointment of a 5–0 loss in the finals to Qatar. One reason the team was so close was that all of the Partners on the team had played Unified football before being chosen for the 1995 World Games team, and the whole group had practiced two nights a week for 10 months. Partner Joshua Makarewicz is in his 11th year of involvement with Special Olympics; he began by helping his parents coach football, then joined a Unified team. That got him so interested in the sport that he made the varsity team at his high school.

"Unified Sports® are a great idea for everyone," said Joshua, a defender. "We all learn from each other. One of the athletes, Luis Ruiz, is like a brother to me. I plan to get certified as a football coach next year, and maybe do Unified skiing up at college in New Hampshire."

A final highlight of the 1995 World Games wore official black and white instead of team colors. Danny Lohr, of Auburn, Washington, USA became the first Special Olympics athlete to serve as a football official at a World Games. Lohr passed all of the necessary exams and was flown to Connecticut to serve as linesman and as field official in some lower division games.

A N   O L Y M P I C   P R O F I L E

When Quico Narvaéz scored two goals to lead the Spanish football team to a 3–2 gold-medal victory over Poland at the 1992 Olympic Summer Games in Barcelona, Spain, the team scored more than a win. It was one of the 18 huge wins that the host country enjoyed after earning only four gold medals in the previous 96 years of the modern Olympic Games! Spain's total medal  count was 22, with 17 more in the three demonstration sports. The Olympic triumph boosted national morale and united a country often divided into bickering ethnic groups. For Spain's "16 days of glory," Basques, Catalans, and Galicians (named for the various regions of Spain) cheered for anyone wearing the Spanish colors!

16 DAYS OF GLORY

Softball

A line drive shoots out to New Jersey shortstop "Big Mike" Margerum. He grabs it and looks to second, where the runner has left for third. A toss to the base puts that runner out. Second-baseman Mike Dixon throws to Curtis Cooper at third. The throw goes wide, but Curtis chases it down and gets it back to Big Mike, covering the base. A triple play to end the game—and New Jersey escapes from a bases-loaded, no-out jam to beat Mexico 12–6!

That triple play was only one highlight of the softball competition at the 1995 World Summer Games. Softball is still the strongest in the United States, but five other countries—Australia, Dominican Republic, Mexico, Panama, and Canada—sent teams to the Games. And for the first time, in 1995, Unified teams competed at World Games.

A close play on the softball diamond.

A N   O L Y M P I C   P R O F I L E

69

Putting
It All
Together:
The Team
Sports

JIM
ABBOTT

Jim Abbott was born without a right hand. But as a boy, he learned to pitch with his left arm and to switch his glove quickly to his left hand to play defense. In 1988, Jim made the U.S. baseball team that would compete at the Summer Olympic Games in Seoul, Korea, where baseball made its first Olympic appearance as a demonstration sport. Jim pitched a full nine innings in the championship game against Japan and made a key defensive play to lead the United States to a 5–3 win and the gold medal. Jim has gone on to a successful professional career, with the California Angels, the New York Yankees, and the Chicago White Sox. In September 1993, he pitched a no-hitter—a rare and treasured achievement for a Major League pitcher—in a 4–0 shut-down of the Cleveland Indians during the Yankees' race for the league championship.

Softball competition pits two 10-player teams against each other, with the extra player generally playing short centerfield. It's slow-pitch softball, with the pitches traveling in an arc between 6 and 12 feet high. Teams of lower ability compete in tee ball, while athletes not ready for team play compete in base running, throwing, fielding, hitting, the base race, bat for distance, and team skills (for teams of five to throw the ball to each other in order).

New Jersey's road to a gold medal at the 1995 World Games was packed with thrills. Along with two triple plays, the team scored a dramatic come-from-behind win over Mexico to make it to the finals. Behind 9–7, the team entered the last inning with the bottom of its order up to bat. Bob Schemelia and Marcus Rutling both tapped singles and ended up on second and third with two outs. Justin Flemingloss got his first hit of the Games to score the two runners and waited on first as the top of the order—Chris Truax, batting .700 for the week—stepped up to the plate. Chris laced a single to left field and Justin ran, eyes fixed on the third base coach. The left-fielder bobbled the ball; Justin ran to third. The throw to the base went high—and Justin ran home, sliding in to beat the tag. New Jersey won, 10–9!

The Illinois Unified team from just outside Chicago brought together players from teams that compete in a small league sponsored by a group of corporations. Partner George and Athlete Paul Kwiecinski are a father-son combination at first base and catcher, while brothers Jody (Partner) and Chuck (athlete) Harris hold down the left- and right-field positions.

Illinois took home a silver medal after a 6–2 loss to Oklahoma in medal game. Some of their tournament highlights were a grand slam home run by Partner Rob Schifrel, an exciting 11–10 win over New Jersey (Unified), and a big improvement in fielding fundamentals.

According to coach Kevin Burke, the idea of Unified softball has been a terrific one for their team. "In the time we've been playing together, I've seen a definite lift in the skill level," said Kevin. "And our corporate league has worked so well, we've become a model for other states to follow."

Volleyball

The spikes fly in Special Olympics volleyball, the youngest of the team sports. Twenty-eight nations sending more than 500 volley-ball athletes to the 1995 World Games show the sport's wide appeal! Volleyball competition includes standard six-a-side games, as well as modified games for athletes of lower ability levels. These games use a slightly smaller court and lower net and lighter ball than regulation volleyball, and they limit the number of points that can be scored before a side-out. (In volley-ball, a team can only earn a point if it served. If the team that didn't serve wins a point, they get the ball to serve and must then win that point to score. A side-out is when the serve switches to the other team and the players rotate for the serve.)

A volleyball match goes to whoever wins 15 points first in two out of three games, or in some competitions, three out of five games. If it sounds like a lot of

A volleyball team sets up for a score.

A N   O L Y M P I C   P R O F I L E

KARCH KIRALY

Even though volleyball was invented in the United States, the U.S. hasn't had much Olympic luck in the sport. An extraordinary player named Karch Kiraly helped to change that at the 1984 and 1988 Olympic Games. Karch had grown up playing the game, and he had the height, strength, and game sense to be considered the best player in the world. After winning the gold medal at the 1984 Olympic Games, Karch and the U.S. team did not lose a single game before entering the competition at the 1988 Olympic Games. They won the gold in Seoul, with Karch as captain. This volleyball legend is now the world's top-ranked beach volleyball player and will try for a spot on the U.S. beach volleyball team that will compete in the 1996 Olympic Games, where the sport makes its Olympic debut.

playing, it is! Peru's women's team at the 1995 World Games made winning look easy, though, with a 15–2/15–1/15–0 sweep of Turkmenistan for the gold medal in their division.

The battle for the bronze medal in that division was another story. South Carolina beat Nebraska in a close match—and Nebraska was thrilled. Not thrilled to lose, but thrilled at how they had played over the week and thrilled with their fourth place finish.

"Those girls were so proud of their play" said Nebraska's chapter director Margaret Lagschulte. "They knew what they had accomplished in winning that ribbon. They all just stepped up several levels of play and gave it their all—giving up their bodies for bumps, pulling together if anyone got down—just becoming a real team."

The team of 10 girls, ages 14 to 23, had been practicing together for a year, but had worked even harder for the two months before the Games. Still, they hadn't played up to their potential until the games against Venezuela, Mexico, and New York to determine what division they should be in.

"They suddenly came together! I said to myself, 'Where have these volleyball players been hiding?'," said head coach Carrie Novotny. "It was like they realized where they were—at an international competition—and they got inspired."

"And the way their eyes glowed when Eunice Kennedy Shriver gave them their ribbons! They said to me, 'You mean this is who started all of Special Olympics? And she's here with us?'."

Carrie has been a Special Olympics volunteer for seven years, as long as her sister Kelley has competed. Kelley played on Nebraska's volleyball team and loved the Games, the Opening Ceremonies, "seeing the stars," and having her sister as a coach. When asked if Carrie is a good coach, Kelley answered, "Heck, yeah!"

Floor Hockey

Floor hockey is the only winter team sport. It is played in a rink but on a floor surface instead of ice. On the playing floor, teams of six, including one goalkeeper, two defenders, and three forwards, compete using a circular felt puck with a center hole and

A N   O L Y M P I C   P R O F I L E

73

Putting
It All
Together:
The Team
Sports

TEAM USA

Like the Special Olympics floor hockey teams that became unlikely champions, the 1980 U.S. Olympic ice hockey team wasn't supposed to triumph at the Winter Olympic Games in Lake Placid, New York, USA. But the team had the right combination of hard-working players, determination, and a goalie named Jim Craig who played the best games of his life—and they put it all together to win. Team USA built up momentum in the early rounds, tying Sweden before beating Czechoslovakia, Norway, Romania, and West Germany. The big test came against four-time Olympic gold-medalist Russia in the semifinals. The Americans fell behind three times before tying it up at 3–3 in the third period. Then it happened. With 10 minutes left, captain Mike Eruzione scored to put the United States ahead. They held off the Soviets as the clock ticked down . . . and they had beaten the Soviets! With that game behind them, they swept into the gold-medal game against Finland and won 4–2. As the television announcer shouted as the clock ticked down to zero in the game against Russia, "Do you believe in miracles?" That week, all of America did.

straight wooden sticks. Unified competition is held for teams with an equal number of Special Olympics athletes and Unified Partners. Athletes of lower ability level compete in the individual skills contest (shoot around the goal, pass, stickhandling, shoot for accuracy, and defense), 10-meter puck dribble, and target shot.

Warm-weather countries such as Jamaica, Brazil, Peru, Zimbabwe, and India welcome the sport of floor hockey as a chance to send athletes to World Winter Games. Jamaica was the first to do so. The floor hockey team that traveled to the 1989 World Games in Reno, Nevada, USA received almost as much national attention as the Jamaican bobsled team that competed in the 1988 Winter Olympic Games in Calgary! In 1993, Jamaica combined with seven other Caribbean countries to send two single-country teams and three combined teams to the World Winter Games in Austria. Team Caribbean once again inspired spectators with its skill and enthusiasm on its way to competition success.

Every sport gives athletes a chance to test their individual skills.

Chapter 9

Special Olympics demonstration sports help expand the opportunities for athletes who may want to try a sport not yet officially part of Special Olympics.

Thomas Edmonds deadlifts 250 kilograms (551 pounds) at the 1995 World Games.

New Opportunities

 Demonstration sports give Special Olympics athletes more choices for training and competing. A sport becomes a demonstration sport when at least six national programs have offered it at their Games for two years and a director is named by Special Olympics International. The sport must also be recognized by the International Olympic Committee (though it doesn't have to be an official Olympic sport) and have an international governing body that will help Special Olympics develop coaches.

Right now, there are five demonstration sports. The other type of non–official Special Olympics sport is a locally popular sport. This is a sport that the organizers of national and state Games want to offer because it is a favorite sport in their area. For example, the 1995 World Games in Connecticut featured sailing and bocce. Cricket is a common locally popular sport in countries that are or were in the British Commonwealth, such as Jamaica, Australia, and South Africa.

Badminton

The sport of badminton is similar to tennis in that players stand across a net from each other and hit an object across with rackets. But for each similarity, there is a difference! The net is raised off the court, which is smaller than a tennis court; the rackets have smaller and lighter heads; and the object hit across is a shuttle (a light, plastic, triangular object) instead of a tennis ball. As in tennis, though, athletes compete in singles, doubles, and mixed doubles. For athletes of lower ability levels, there are the skills tests of target serve, target stroke, and return serve. Badminton is popular in Special Olympics programs in the Asia/Pacific region, such as those in Bangladesh, Hong Kong, and Singapore; in European countries such as Austria, France, and Kazakhstan; and in the United States.

Golf

To judge by the number of athletes joining the ranks of Special Olympics golf programs, golf is hot. It's a sport that more and more athletes are discovering they can play well and enjoy with family and friends. Through the United States Golf Association (USGA) and Professional Golfers Association of America (PGA), club professionals around the United States hold training schools for coaches and clinics for athletes, helping to raise the quality of play.

Special Olympics golf challenges athletes' concentration and skill.

Athletes can progress through three levels of competition. Individual skills contests (short putt, long putt, chipping, pitching, iron shot, and wood shot) score for accuracy and distance. Partners team competition, which helps Special Olympics golfers learn golf rules and *etiquette*, pairs two coaches with two athletes for a nine-hole tournament. Level 3 athletes compete in 18-hole stroke play tournaments, with each division scored using the golfers' *handicaps*.

Powerlifting

Powerlifting is a simple sport. You either lift the weight, or you don't. You train and train and train and when the competition comes, you put your hands on the bar and you lift with every bit of strength you have. If you've prepared your body and your mind, you lift the bar clean. You keep lifting until you are beyond your best—and the weight you can't lift becomes your goal for the next competition.

It may sound simple, but the hours of hoisting weights and learning technique, and the importance of believing in your ability, aren't simple at all. Special Olympics athletes have shown that they have what it takes to excel at this demanding sport, and powerlifting competitions are packed with thrills and personal triumphs.

There are three Special Olympics powerlifting events: the benchpress, in which an athlete lies on his or her back on a bench and lifts a bar loaded with weights up from the chest; the deadlift,

Gary Jelen was the first Special Olympics power-lifter in the United Kingdom.

in which an athlete lifts a loaded bar up from the floor in one continuous motion until the lifter is standing straight up; and the squat, in which an athlete stands with the bar behind his or her head then squats down and stands back up. The combination adds weights lifted in the deadlift and benchpress, and the score in the triple combination is the results in all three lifts added together. Athletes of lower ability level compete in modified push-ups, sit-ups, and exercycle.

The top lifters in Special Olympics amaze spectators with their strength. Nine years ago, Gary Jelen became the first young man with mental retardation to train in powerlifting in England. The 198-pounder's best lift was a 450-pound deadlift at a demonstration in the United States in May 1993. Because of this pioneer, more than 500 athletes now participate in Special Olympics powerlifting in England. New Jersey's Donald Pyscaty began weight training years ago, as

Special Olympics athletes of all ages benefit from strength training.

a way to lose weight and improve his health. As one of the first Special Olympics "big lifters," Donald lifted 385 pounds in the bench press and 418 pounds in the deadlift to win both events and the combined medal at the 1991 World Games.

At the 1995 World Games, top lifters in the 114-pound class were Aaron Hayman of Hawaii, USA, with gold medals in the squat, deadlift (292 pounds), and triple combination; and Saba Al Shaktari of Kuwait with a 198-pound gold-medal lift in the benchpress. In the 198-pound class, Richard Davis of Nebraska, USA topped his division with a triple combination of 1,377 pounds: 507 in the squat, 297 in the benchpress, and 573 in the deadlift! Tiny Sheri Lyn Johnston of Louisiana, USA led the 30 female competitors by lifting more than five times her body weight, with lifts of 203.75 pounds (squat), 253.75 pounds (deadlift), and 126.75 pounds (benchpress), totalling 584 pounds.

Bart Conner and Andy Leonard at a White House sports celebration.

Powerlifting success stories are not complete without Andy Leonard. Andy came to the United States from South Vietnam in 1975, orphaned by the Vietnam War. Andy was adopted by the Leonard family, who soon discovered that the many ear infections Andy had had in Vietnam caused brain damage. Throughout his school years, he had problems reading and writing and was in special education classes in high school. But even though he was smaller than most other students—Andy is five feet tall and weighs 111 pounds—he had a lot of athletic talent.

"I have never met an athlete, either amateur or professional, who has the fortitude of Andy Leonard.... He is the perfect example of human spirit."

—Clyde Doll, powerlifting coach

When Andy was 16, a teacher suggested that he try Special Olympics. Andy trained in track and won a gold medal in the pentathlon at the Pennsylvania State Games in 1988. Then his coach introduced him to her husband, Clyde Doll, a powerlifter. The rest is history.

Andy impressed Clyde with his strength and work habits. He soon was competing, not only in Special Olympics powerlifting competitions, but also in competitions sponsored by the American Drug Free Powerlifting Association (ADFPA). He won the 114-pound title at the ADFPA's Lifetime Drug Free Contest in 1994 and 1995 and became the first Special Olympics athlete to win a U.S. title for people without disabilities! In 1991, Andy achieved a then-personal best dead lift of 402.5 pounds to earn a gold medal in his class at the Special Olympics World Summer Games—even though he had smashed his finger with a weight plate just before his lift!

If you ask Andy why he likes powerlifting, he's quick with the answer. "Powerlifting makes my body stronger and my muscles bigger," he said. "Because of my powerlifting I have gone on trips and met a lot of people. People know me and come to my meets to cheer. I've made friends in Special Olympics and we go to movies and go bowling. I'm going to keep training, and I would also like to help Clyde coach other athletes."

Andy wowed the crowd at the powerlifting events at the 1995 World Games as a guest lifter. He lifted 413 pounds in the deadlift, 352 pounds in the squat, and 226 pounds in the benchpress—with the squat, the benchpress, and the triple total of 901 pounds topping his personal bests!

"Andy is one of the top lifters in his weight in the United States," said Clyde Doll. "He's 27 years old now and he's still getting stronger. If they ever included powerlifting events in the Olympic Games (instead of the weightlifting events of the snatch and the clean-and-jerk), he would make the team.

"I have never met an athlete, either amateur or professional, who has the fortitude of Andy Leonard. Any powerlifting gym in the country knows of his accomplishments. He is the perfect example of the human spirit."

Table Tennis

Speedy hands and quick reactions will get an athlete far in the sport of table tennis. Tough competition at the 1995 World Games showcased 170 athletes from 50 countries—a huge increase from the 12 athletes that competed at the 1987 World Games. The countries competing show in what parts of the world the sport is most popular. Ten teams were from the Asia/Pacific region, nine represented republics of the former Soviet Union, and 16 more hailed from Europe.

Table tennis is a game of speed and coordination.

Table tennis events include singles, doubles, mixed doubles, and individual skills contests. The target serve, racquet bounce, and return shot challenge the skills of athletes with lower abilities.

Team Handball

Team handball combines elements of basketball and football to create a fast-paced, exciting sport. Two teams of seven compete on a basketball-size court with a goal cage at each end. Players can move the ball by passing, dribbling, carrying it for up to three steps, or advancing it with their body—except with their legs below the knee. Defending players can also use their bodies to block an opponent with or without the ball. Team handball demands excellent all-around physical skills and a good

Going for the ball in a fast-paced team handball game.

memory for rules and strategies! Special Olympics athletes compete in seven-a-side games or in non-contact five-a-side games. The three individual skills contests for athletes of lower ability levels are target pass, 10-meter dribble and shoot.

For three years now, Special Olympics athletes have competed right along with teams from all over the United States in the U.S. Team Handball Federation National Tournament. The top finish by a team was fifth, in 1994. After the 1995 tournament, Natshia Hardrick of Alabama Special Olympics was named to the United States select team and competed for the South at the Olympic Festival in August 1995—the first Special Olympics athlete to be named to a national team.

Chapter 10

*Good habits and
hard work build
success in all
athletes.*

Eric Tosado of
Puerto Rico ran
the 100-meter dash
in 11.3 seconds in
1987.

Building Success, Day by Day

 In the Ancient Olympic Games, champions were crowned with a wreath from a sacred olive tree at Olympus. An olive wreath and today's Olympic gold medal surely symbolize success. But the word *success* can mean many different things to people. While it often means reaching the top and being recognized as the best, the Special Olympics athletes featured in this book show us many other ways to have a successful life.

What would their definition of *success* be? Success is working hard to reach your potential. It's setting and achieving goals. It's building your character with self-confidence, consideration for others, and excitement for life. It's simply learning to do your best in all things, even if you face obstacles or small failures. Success is believing that you will succeed—that victory belongs to you!

Peggy Anderson coaches lower ability athletes in northern Virginia, USA. She knows that sports success comes at many levels. "If you don't expect anything, you don't get anything," said Peggy. "I set goals for my athletes and I give them all I've got, and they give all they can. That's success for them."

Peggy tells of athlete Anne Finney, who just wouldn't run. "I'd work and work, but every chance she'd get, she'd just go sit in a corner. Sometimes I would grab her arm and make her move with me. She liked basketball and I told her that the speed dribble event means running. Well, we worked some more and I took her to the State Games, and she took that ball and ran! And then she ran around the bases in softball skills! That was a happy girl standing up to get her medals!"

To succeed in anything—school, sports, art, music—you have to work very hard. In sports, that means:

- learning all that you can about your sport,
- training for that sport,
- maintaining good eating and sleeping habits,
- keeping your body fit, and
- having fun!

These things are true for athletes who compete in their community baseball or

softball leagues, for Olympic and professional athletes, and for Special Olympics athletes. A winning lifestyle usually takes sacrifice. It also takes teamwork, like family and friends who help an athlete maintain healthy habits.

Colorado, USA's Mike and Mark Hembd are twins who have trained together in Special Olympics sports since they were eight years old. By the time they were in their twenties and holding down good jobs in electronic assembly, they were working out every night after work, lifting weights, running, or swimming. They played basketball, softball, or soccer one night a week, and they skied every Saturday during the winter.

With all of this training, they knew they had to eat right. Several years before, the twins had put on a weightlifting demonstration with Arnold Schwarzenegger. He encouraged them to keep working

Success in sports means hard work—but it also means fun.

out and also told them to stay away from junk food. So Mark and Mike never eat things like potato chips that have a lot of fat and not many nutrients. Every other night they treat themselves to a low-fat dessert like frozen yogurt.

The Hembd twins have succeeded in sports because they work hard and help each other and because of the support of their parents. The Hembd family was named Colorado Special Olympics Family of the Year in 1992 for their volunteer work and leadership contributions.

Another family "team" lives across the Atlantic Ocean from the Hembd family, in Brussels, Belgium. Of the six children in the VanOrmelingen family, three are Special Olympics athletes. Bart, age 32, competed in football at the 1987 World Games and in the half marathon at the 1991 and 1995 World Games. According to Bart's mother Mimi, who has headed up Family Programs in Belgium and in Europe, sports helped turn her shy boy into one of the best-known figures in their neighborhood!

Bart VanOrmelingen, "one of the best-known figures in his neighborhood."

"Special Olympics is more than a part of Bart's life," Mimi said. "It is his life . . . it's all about sports, training and competition." Bart runs 6 to 12 kilometers (about 4 to 8 miles) each evening after he finishes his day's work at a sheltered workshop. Between running, swimming, and playing football, sports and Special Olympics give Bart a very active and healthy lifestyle. He has learned to set goals and work toward them; he's learned to enjoy friends and fellow athletes like Wim Broothaers, with whom he runs in a local running club; and he's learned to use his fluency in Dutch, French, and English to meet even more people!

As for his mother, she won't be satisfied until every Special Olympics family is cheering at competitions and supporting their athlete's training habits at home!

"My goals in Special Olympics are to be a winner, and the best I can be. I want to make my coaches and peers proud of me. Winning is not everything, although it is more fun. My family is always there to support me and help me go the extra mile, so to speak."

—Brian Pountain,
Special Olympics athlete

Chapter 11

Many Olympic and Special Olympics athletes succeed in areas other than sports.

Cyclists celebrate a great race.

Champions in Life

 Building a successful lifestyle and working hard in sports can really help you in other parts of your life. If you're a student, the discipline from training and following rules can help you learn better. If you work at a job, your physical skills, coordination, and memory can improve with sports and help you in your work. Sports give you confidence and can teach you to take chances. Sports also help you make friends and show you how to get along with many different people.

For some Olympic and Special Olympics athletes, sports have really opened doors to success in other areas. Norwegian figure skater Sonja Henie won gold medals at the 1928, 1932, and 1936 Winter Olympic Games. She turned her sports success into an acting career, making 11 films between 1938 and 1960. American swimming star Johnny Weismuller, a five-time gold medal winner at the 1924 and 1928 Olympic Games, also went on to star in the movies—as Tarzan!

Chris Burke was a Special Olympics athlete in New York State, USA. He always dreamed of being an actor, and competing in sports helped give him the confidence to pursue his dream. Chris was chosen to appear in a television movie and did so well that the director of the movie decided to put him in a television series. The show, "Life Goes On," ran for four years on the ABC network.

**Actor Chris Burke with Eunice
Kennedy Shriver.**

Some athletes become leaders in the sports field. Jean-Claude Killy of France, who won three gold medals in Alpine skiing in 1968, was copresident of the 1992 Winter Olympic Games in Albertville, France. Former American Olympians Tom McMillen (basketball) and Florence Griffith-Joyner (track) serve as cochairpeople of the President's Council on Physical Fitness and Sports. One of their goals is to improve the fitness habits of young people in America.

American swimmer Mary T. Meagher made a commitment to using her success in sports to help others. Mary won three Olympic gold medals in 1984 and a silver and bronze in 1988. The tenth of 11 children, Mary has always counted on the help and support of her big family. She in turn chooses leadership roles, serving as the national athlete representative for U.S. swimming and the swimming representative to the U.S. Olympics Committee's Athlete Advisory Council. She's been a member of the board of directors of both the U.S. Olympic Committee and Special Olympics International. In all of these activities, Mary works to help others get as much out of sports as she has.

"Having a successful swimming career has given me a base to build my life on," said Mary. "With the confidence I gained through my successes—and failures—I don't feel like I have anything to prove in life—just a whole lot of things I want to do."

Like Mary, Special Olympics athlete Kevin Hartley is recognized for his outstanding career in sports and community service. In 1992, he was named to the Arizona Governor's Council for Physical Fitness and Sports. Kevin has competed in Special Olympics since he was 12 years old. Of the many sports he plays, his favorite is basketball. He plays in a church league and competed in Unfied basketball at the 1995 World Games.

In 1992, Kevin became the first Arizona Special Olympics athlete to finish the Phoenix Marathon, in a time of 3 hours 53 minutes. He received varsity letters in high school track for two years. He has also trained with a group that hikes the Grand Canyon from rim to rim—22 miles.

"Special Olympics athletes can actually participate in life rather than standing on the sidelines."

—Christi Todd,
Special Olympics Athletes for Outreach

Kevin recently moved from his job at McDonalds to the County Flood Control crew. His new job doesn't leave much time for speaking as an Athlete for Outreach, but he's glad to be out in the real world. In 1992, Kevin was chosen to introduce athlete and movie star Arnold Schwarzenegger—who was then the chairperson of the President's Council on Physical Fitness and Sports—to a crowd of students and teachers at a local school. But it was Kevin who was in the spotlight when Schwarzenegger raised Kevin's hand above his head and said, "I'd like to introduce you to a hero of mine, Kevin Hartley!"

Another area where athletes can shine is in politics. One example is Olympic basketball player Bill Bradley. After starring on the gold-medal men's basketball team in the 1964 Tokyo Olympics, Bill went on to play 10 seasons with the NBA's New York Knicks, leading them to two glorious NBA Championships. Since 1978, he has represented New Jersey in the U.S. Senate.

Stephen Sellows also felt called to go into public service. He was a Special Olympics athlete in Washington, D.C. for many years and competed in the 1968 and 1970 World Games. Stephen began speaking out about the rights of people with disabilities and was named to the D.C. Mayor's Committee for Persons with Disabilities. In addition to his regular job, and the letter writing and public speaking that being on the committee requires, he volunteered in a D.C. councilman's office.

Doing your best and reaching for the top—that's success!

These are only some of the athletes who do exciting and important things. In every town, there are Special Olympics athletes who truly reach their potential in every part of their lives. Athletes succeed as, among other things, musicians, painters, volunteers, and employees. They compete in school and community sports programs. In road races and marathons around the world, Special Olympics athletes are crossing the finish line. They believe they can succeed, and they do succeed. Family and friends believe in them, too. The power of believing in your ability is a great lesson to learn!

Special Olympics— Opening Doors!

Special Olympics does so many things. It offers sports training in 22 different sports. It provides fair competition that gives people with mental retardation a chance to show the world what they can do. It brings people together to make a difference in the lives of Special Olympics athletes, families, and volunteers.

Maybe what Special Olympics does best, though, is open doors. It opens doors to people of all ages with mental retardation, inviting them to come in and to become faster, to go higher, and to feel stronger. Its doors are also open for other people to learn how able a person with disabilities can be.

Mike Owen, a Unified Sports® basketball coach in Evansville, Indiana, can see how Special Olympics opens doors between his athletes with and without mental retardation. He said, "Winning a close game and seeing the players smile, seeing them lose with character—it just knocks the door wide open and gets us all closer together as a group."

Perhaps Special Olympics coaches and organizers are happiest when their athletes take their new skills, strength, and discipline and go succeed in the world. Maybe an athlete bursts from the "doors" of Special Olympics to stand up and receive a high school diploma, varsity sports letter, or Employee of the Month honors at work!

Or maybe, Special Olympics helps athletes like Andy Leonard or Natshia Hardrick pursue a dream of competing in the Olympic Games. And this brings us back to where we started—celebrating all of the athletes with "hearts of gold," who show the world true Olympic Spirit.

Skill, courage, sharing, and joy—the spirit of Special Olympics!

Chad Oncale scored a gold-medal total of 116.90 points in the all-around at his first World Games in 1987.

How You Can Be Part of Special Olympics

Anyone who loves sports can be part of Special Olympics. If you are eligible to be a Special Olympics athlete (that is, if you have mental retardation), you can train and compete in the sports that are offered by your local Special Olympics program. Your coach will help you learn the skills that you need and set goals—and soon you will be competing!

Some Special Olympics athletes choose to take a break from competing and help out as a coaching assistant or volunteer. Athlete Chad Oncale of Louisiana, USA began sharing his gymnastics expertise when he was still in his teens. Leonard Weirich and Kristen Doherty of Maryland, USA know how important good coaches are to their Special Olympics experience, so they bring their excellent sports background to athletes in track and swimming.

If you are not eligible to be a Special Olympics athlete, you have several ways to become involved. You can learn how to be a volunteer coach. You can also choose to be a coaching assistant. Or you can volunteer on the day of the Special Olympics Games in your area: you can be an athlete escort, a runner for the officials, or you can cheer on the athletes!

"When I'm competing, I feel fantastic and great and nervous."

—Chad Oncale,
Special Olympics athlete

Another great choice is to join a Unified Sports® team. You need to check with your local Special Olympics program to see if there is a Unified Sports® league in your area. If there isn't, maybe you can help start one!

Many school systems also have Sports Partnerships programs, in which athletes with mental retardation train alongside varsity and junior varsity athletes and then compete in Special Olympics events at varsity and junior varsity competitions. In Partners Clubs®, high school students are matched with a Special Olympics athlete and help the athlete train in sports, but they also share social and recreational activities.

To learn about the Special Olympics program in your state—or to find out how you can meet a Special Olympics athlete in your area—call Special Olympics International at 1-800-700-8585 and they will tell you how to call your local program!

776 B.C.	First record of the ancient Olympic Games
393 B.C.	Last of the ancient Olympic Games
394 B.C.	Roman emperor decrees that there will be no more Olympic Games
1766	Discovery of Olympia by English archeologist Richard Chandler
1881	Discovery of records of the Olympic Games
1894	Baron Pierre de Coubertin launches Olympic movement
1896	First modern Olympic Games held in Athens, Greece
1913	A drawing of five interlocking rings is discovered in Greece; de Coubertin makes this the Olympic emblem
1916	No Olympic Games because of World War I
1922	Olympic motto adopted: "Citius, Altius, Fortius"
1924	First Olympic Winter Games held in Chamonix, France
1938	African-American Jesse Owens wins four gold medals at Olympic Games in Berlin, upsetting Adolf Hitler
1940, 1944	No Olympic Games because of World War II
1962	Eunice Kennedy Shriver starts Camp Shriver
1968	First Special Olympics Games held in Chicago, Illinois, USA
1972	American swimmer Mark Spitz wins seven gold medals
1972	Tragedy strikes the Munich Olympic Games when Arab terrorists kidnap and later kill Israeli athletes and coaches
1980	The United States refuses to attend the Moscow Olympic Games in protest of the Soviet Union's invasion of Afghanistan
1984	The Soviet Union refuse to attend the Los Angeles Games in retaliation for the U.S. boycott in 1980
1987	The International Olympic Committee officially recognizes and endorses Special Olympics International
1988	Olympic Games in Seoul are first to include professional athletes
1992	First Olympic Games after dissolution of Soviet Union. Former republics compete on their own or join with "Unified Team"
1993	First World Special Olympics Games held outside the United States, with Winter Games in Salzburg and Schladming, Austria
1994	First time Olympic Winter Games held two years after Summer Games, in Lillehammer, Norway
1996	Centennial Olympic Games to be held in Atlanta, Georgia, USA
1997	Special Olympics World Winter Games to be held in Toronto/ Collingwood, Ontario, in Canada.
1999	Special Olympics World Summer Games to be held in Raleigh/ Durham/Chapel Hill, North Carolina, USA.

apparatus The equipment used for different gymnastics routines.

downhill The fastest and longest Alpine skiing event.

dressage An equestrian event in which the horse and rider move through a set sequence of moves, including a walk, trot, and cantor. They are judged on the precision and fluidity of their movements.

equitation An equestrian event in which the rider moves the horse through walking and trotting; judged on body position and control of the horse.

etiquette The expected behavior and good form required in a certain setting.

fetal alcohol syndrome A condition in a baby whose mother drank alcoholic beverages while she was pregnant. A baby with this condition often has mental retardation, other developmental disabilities, or possibly more severe or physical disabilities.

fitness conditioning Working your body to make your muscles, heart, and lungs strong and to make your joints and muscles flexible.

handicap In the sport of golf, a number given to a golfer based on his or her usual score relative to par. (Par is the number of strokes it should take to play 18 holes on any given course.) When you play in a tournament, your handicap is used to help you evenly compete with other golfers. Handicaps are also used in the sport of bowling.

heat A grouping of athletes for a preliminary competition that leads to a final.

inclusion The act of enabling a person with a disability to participate in the activities of people without disabilities on a regular basis.

motor skills The basic physical skills that make up all of our actions: moving our arms, legs, and fingers in order to complete a task.

prix caprilli An English equestrian event that combines the dressage with small jumps; riders and their mounts are judged on their fluidity as they proceed through the required moves.

showmanship An equestrian event in which an athlete on foot demonstrates a horse's movements and posture by presenting, turning, and walking it around.

slalom The shortest Alpine skiing event, in which the athlete must ski around a series of gates (a gate consists of two sets of two poles with a panel between the poles) set in a zig-zag pattern down a hill.

sportsmanship Being a fair competitor, a generous loser, and a graceful winner.

therapeutic Intended to treat a temporary or permanent disability. Therapeutic sports programs work to develop both physical abilities and confidence.

volunteers People who perform a job without being paid for it.

For Further Reading

About Special Olympics

Brown, Fern. *Special Olympics.* New York: Franklin Watts, 1992.

Gilbert, Nancy. *The Special Olympics.* Mankato, MN: Creative Education, 1990.

Spirit Magazine. Washington, DC: Special Olympics International.

About the Olympics Games

Duder, Tessa. *Journey to Olympia: The Story of the Ancient Olympics.* New York: Scholastic, 1992.

Knight, Theodore. *The Olympic Games.* San Diego: Lucent Books, 1991.

About Sports

Allen, Anne. *Sports for the Handicapped.* New York: Walker & Co., 1981

Schwarzenegger, Arnold, with Charles Gaines. *Arnold's Fitness for Kids.* New York: Doubleday, 1993.

Schneider, Tom. *Everybody's a Winner: A Kid's Guide to New Sports and Fitness.* Boston: Little Brown, 1976.

Sports Illustrated for Kids Magazine. New York: Times Inc.

Source List

Johnson, William Oscar. *The Olympics: A History of the Games.* New York: Time, Inc. Magazine Co. with Oxmoor House Inc., 1992.

Kieran, John, and Arthur Daley. *The Story of the Olympic Games, 776 B.C. to 1972.* Philadelphia: J. B. Lippincott Co., 1973.

Killanin, Lord, and John Rodda. *The Olympic Games.* New York: Macmillan Publishing Co., 1980.

Special Olympics International. *Special Olympics Sports Rules Book (Winter and Summer),* Washington, DC: Special Olympics International.

Sports Illustrated Magazine. New York: Time, Inc.

Wallenchinsky, Dave. *The Complete Book of the Olympics.* Boston: Little Brown & Co., 1991.

Note: Pages in italics refer to pictures and tables.

Sheila Dinn has experience as a sportswriter, a newspaper columnist, and a staff member for Special Olympics International headquarters. Dinn's work with Special Olympics athletes and their families led her to write this book for them.